Problems and Solutions of Teaching English

PROBLEMS AND SOLUTIONS OF TEACHING ENGLISH

Ram Kumar Sharma

Commonwealth

Problems and Solutions of Teaching English

Edition : 2016

ISBN 81-7169-038-6

Published by :
COMMONWEALTH PUBLISHERS PVT. LTD.
4831/24, Prahlad Street,
Ansari Road, Darya Ganj,
New Delhi - 110002
Ph. : 23272541, 23257835
Fax : 91- 011- 23257835
e-mail : commonwealthbooks@gmail.com

Laser Typesetting by :
Stylish Laser Typesetter
Delhi - 110053

Printed at :
Roshan Offset Printers
Delhi

Dedicated

to

My Parents

Preface

Even after more than three decades have passed since Britishers left India, English occupies a place of prestige in our country. People belonging not only to different language groups but also to the same speech community make use of English in their inter-personal communication. In big metropolises of India, it is really difficult to come across any educated person who can speak any Indian language well without avoiding the use of English words. Surprisingly, however, the number of people who can speak and write English correctly is receding day by day in India in general and Bihar in particular. The bilingual, trilingual and multilingual situations in India in general and Bihar in particular have made it a challenging job to teach English as a second language which is at once essential and arduous.

I have tried to investigate the problems related to English language teaching in Bihar. In the first chapter, I have examined in a historical perspective the varying roles and uses of psycholinguistic implications of teaching English in Bihar have been discussed. I have also examined the impact of Bihar Government legislations regarding teaching of English formulated from time to time. The persistence of the so-called 'U' and non 'U' social strata disrupts the smoothness of English teaching in Bihar. In the third chapter, the problems of teaching English in Middle and High Schools have been discussed. The problems dealt with in this chapter are the standard in which the teaching of English should begin, misconceptions regarding English language teaching, faulty teaching methods, unpalatable textbooks and their mishandling, etc. In the fourth chapter, I have discussed the problems of teaching English in the colleges of Bihar, where the method of teaching is faulty and the selection of teaching items improper. The teaching of English at this stage is mistaken to be the teaching of English literature only and the points of linguistic interest are generally ignored. It has been suggested, therefore, that a language oriented syllabus should at once be introduced to the teaching of English in the colleges of Bihar. In the fifth chapter, I have discussed the problems which both the students and teachers in Training Colleges in Bihar are faced with. It is in these colleges where the future school teachers of English are imparted training. The training programme appears to be theoretical only. The student-teachers, even after receiving training from these colleges, remain ignorant of the effectiveness and limitations of teaching aids. In the sixth chapter, I have discussed the problems of teaching English pronunciation to the students of Bihar, who face difficulty in picking up correct pronunciation of English. They first learn how to articulate the sounds of their dialects, *i.e.*, Magahi or Bhojpuri, Maithili or Santhali etc., followed by the sounds of their language, *i.e.* Hindi. English is the third language they learn and, thus, the sounds of the language they have already acquired interfere with their pronunciation of English. The seventh chapter sums up the whole discussion and suggests ways and measures to resolve the problems of teaching English as a second language in Bihar.

I have collected relevant information from all over Bihar. Questionnaires were prepared and were circulated to be filled up by the Heads of Institutions, teachers of English and the students of the schools and colleges of Bihar. I visited a large number of schools and colleges situated in different parts of Bihar to have a through acquaintance with and discussion on the problems of teaching English in Bihar. The opinions of those interviewed, besides their answers to the questionnaires, helped me in proper evaluation of the problems. Materials for the research-work were collected from various sources *(i)* Books—most of them referred to in the Bibliography, *(ii)* Journals, *(iii)* Reports, *(iv)* Information from newspapers, magazines etc. The views and ideas of the scholars in the field of Linguistics and Language Teaching and my practical experience as a teacher of English have helped me in understanding the problems of the students and teachers of English.

I am greatly indebted to Dr. A.K. Sharma, P.G.

Department of English, Bhagalpur University, Bhagalpur but for whose careful guidance and close supervision, it would have been impossible for me to complete this study.

I would like to express my deep sense of gratitude to Dr. K.M. Tiwari, Professor of English, Patna University, Patna for his encouragement and guidance and to Dr. R.K. Sinha, Retired Professor and Head, Department of English, Patna University, Patna, Dr. D.D. Sharma, Professor and Head, Department of English and European Languages, Lucknow University, Lucknow, Dr. R.C. Prasad, Professor and Head, Department of English, Patna University, Patna, Dr. D. Thakur, Professor of English, University of Sanna, Yemen, Arab Republic, Dr. A.K. Sinha, Reader and Head of the Department of Linguistics, Delhi University, Delhi, Sri A.P. Sharma, Administrative Officer, Patna Museum for their blessings and encouragement.

My grateful thanks are due to Dr. Govinda Prasad Singh, Head of the Dept. of English, S.P.M. College, Biharsharif, Dr. D.K. Singh, Prof. and Head of the Dept. of English of our College and Mr. B.K. Verma and Mrs. Manju Sinha both my colleagues and Dr. R.P. Sharma, Lecturer, Dept. of Hindi, T.N.B. College, Bhagalpur for their encouraging suggestions.

My heartfelt thanks are due to the librarians of Delhi University Library, Delhi, National Library, Calcutta, Patna University Library, Patna, British Library, Patna, CIEFL, Regional Centre Library, Lucknow, Bhagalpur University Library, Bhagalpur, Bihar Legislative Assembly Library, Patna, Patna Secretariat Library, Patna, Ram Krishna Mission Library, Patna, who helped me with efficiency and courtesy.

My grateful thanks are due to Messers Janaki Prakashan and especially to Mr. Nand Kishore Singh for his willingness to publish the book under his own personal supervision.

Ram Kumar Sharma

Contents

1 Introduction

After Independence, when the educationists and the policy makers felt the necessity for reorientation of our educational policy, there was a strong opinion in some of the Indian educational sectors in favour of eliminating English or relegating it to a very subordinate place. There was a bitter controversy with regard to the place of English in system of education and there has been due to this a constant change of decisions as to what position English should hold in the present set up. Some states demanded that English should be retained as link language or the official language, apart from being the language or international communication. Some other states, on the other hand, deliberately attempted to undermine the importance of the study of English. Some educationists maintained that talents could develop through mother tongues and, thus, there was no need for devoting time and energy in learning a language which was foreign to our culture. The reason, they felt, was that the use of a language other than the mother tongue as the medium of instruction inhibited psychologically the development of children. Educationally, it was thought to be a wastage of time and distortion of knowledge. The opinions of M.K. Gandhi (1916)[1] and the Punjab University Enquiry Committee of 1932-33[2] were echoed by many educationists and educational bodies after Independence. "Learning through the mother tongue is the most potent and comprehensive medium for the expression of the student's entire personality" was the declaration of the Secondary Education Commission

1. M.K. Gandhi, *The Problem of Education* (Ahmedabad : Navjivan Press, 1962), p. 4.
2. Quoted in S.N. Chib, *Language, University and Nationalism in India* (Mysore : Oxford University Press, 1936), pp. 25-26.

1956.[3] "No foreign language", said G.R. Sharma, "Can take the place of the mother tongue and no system of education can afford to disregard it without serious deriment to the mental development of the child. ...The child think and dreams in the language through which he acquires the earliest firsthand experiences of life. This naturally happens to be the mother tongue. And for this reason the mother tongue becomes the first condition of schooling for the intellectual development of the child".[4] These arguments for the mother tongue as the medium of instruction in schools and colleges appear to have rested more on the attitudes to language of the students, and the deficiencies of the teachers, than on any positive benefits of such instruction, for as the report goes, the failures in both arts and science faculties in Nagpur University in 1955 were higher among the regional medium students than the English medium students.[5] These arguments, therefore, were more political than educational or psychological.

It is true that even after more than four decades since Britishers left India, English occupies a place of prestige in our country. No indigenous language howsoever has come up to replace English either as a medium of communication or as an official language. This is not due to the fact that English alone can be the language of government, law, education or technology. On the contrary, "any language is as good as any other language, in the sense that every language is equally well adopted to the uses to which the community puts... All languages are equally capable of being developed for all purposes and no language is any less qualified to be the vehicle of modern science and technology than were English and Russian some centuries ago."[6]

English in India : Pre-Independence Period

Due to historical reasons, English has come to occupy a dominant place in India. At one time, the different parts of

---

3. Report of the Secondary Education Commission (Govt. of India, 1956, Chapt. V).
4. G.R. Sharma, 'The Teacher of Hindi' in *Shiksha* (April 1957), p. 148.
5. Reported in *The Times of India* (5 January 1956), p. 6.
6. M.A.K. Halliday, Angus McIntosh and Peter Strevens, *The Linguistic Sciences and Language Teaching* (London : ELBS & Longman Group Ltd., 1966), p. 101.

the sub-continent (India, Pakistan, Ceylon and Burma) were able to join through the medium of English under British Empire. When the British first came to India after the incorporation of the East India Company in 1600, they brought with them not only the tools of trade and the implements of war, but also their language and literature. At first, they were forced to learn indigenous language to carry on the business of commerce and the tasks of administration. They had no permanent interest in the country with the Mugal rule in total disintegration. "At no period of its history has India been an altogether unenlightened country".[7]

British administrators cared little for the cultural wants of the Indian millions. "It was inevitable that culture should be in jeopardy and civilization at its lowest ebb : no wonder eighteenth century India was culturally little than a waste land".[8]

Britishers did not want the spread of European type of education in India. They felt that 'western' education would enable Indians to challenge the alien rule as was the case with America. "We had just lost America from our own folly in having allowed the establishment of schools and colleges and that it would not do for us to repeat the same act of folly in this regard to India".[9] And when they turned to promote the education of Indians, it was a political necessity that made them do so. They adopted orientalism or encouragement of classical learning for their educational policy[10] which was opposed by the missionaries, like Charles Grant (1746-1823) whose plan was to teach English to the people of India.[11]

Meanwhile, a controversy arose between 'Anglicists' and 'Orientalists'. I withheld the smooth progress of English in

7. Vincet A. Smith, *The Oxford History of India* (London : Oxford University Press), p. 367.
8. Suniti Kumar Chatterjee (ed.), *The Cultural Heritage of India,* Volume V (Languages and Literatures) Calcutta : Ram Krishna Mission, Institute of Culture), p. 458.
9. Parliamentary Papers 1852-53, XXXII, p. 113.
10. Amarnath Basu, *Education in Modern India* (Calcutta : Orient Book Company), pp. 13-14.
11. Henry Sharp (ed.), *Selections from Educational Records* (Calcutta : Superintendent of Government Printing, 1920), pp. 81-83.

India. The 'Orientalists' advocated a revival of Sanskrit and Persian learning. But the noted Hindu leaders like Raja Ram Mohan Roy and Christian missionaries like William Carey advocated western education through the medium of English. This missionary effort was powerfully supported by those progressive Hindus who symbolised "a new-found desire on the part of the natives of India for a share in the knowledge and training which they discerned to be a large part of the secret of the superior efficiency of the nations from the west, and the source of what was strong and admirable in English character".[12] Then there were members of the middle class. They saw that a capacity to speak and write English, which was the language of the rulers, was necessary for lucrative posts under government. It provided a decent income and an important status in society. The voices of the people could not be silenced.

Raja Ram Mohan Roy took the issue with all seriousness. He was against Oriental policy of education. When a proposal by General Committee of Public Instruction for founding a Sanskrit College in Calcutta was put forward, he wrote to Lord Amherst on the 11th December 1913, "the Sanskrit system of education would be the best calculated to keep this country in darkness if such had been the policy of the British legislator. But as the improvement of the native population is the object of the government, it will consequently promote a more liberal and enlightened system of instruction, embracing Mathematics, natural philosophy, chemistry and anatomy with other useful sciences which may be accomplished by employing a few gentlemen of talents and learning educated in Europe, and providing a college furnished with necessary books, instruments and other apparatus".[13]

A still greater attack was made on the work of the committee by the Directors themselves. They not only felt the superiority of English education, they even expressed the view that the teaching of mere Hindu or Mohammedan literature meant the teaching of "a great deal of what was frivolous, no

12. H.R. James, *Education and Statesmanship in India 1797-1910* (London Longmans, 1952). p. 14.
13. Henry Sharp (ed.), *op. cit.*, p. 101.

a little of what was purely mischievous and a small reminder indeed in which utility was in any way concerned".[14]

The sharp differences brought the work of the Committee to a standstill and Lord Macaulay was appointed the President of the committee in 1834. His main contention was that the study of English could be beneficial to those Indians who were pursuing higher studies than Arabic and Sanskrit. He pointed out that there was already an effective demand for English. He argued that "since indigenous languages were inadequate and chaotic, and indigenous arts and literature were petty futile things. Only 'Western' education with English as the sole medium would deliver the good".[15] He hopefully thought that "if our plan of education are followed up, there would not be a single idolater among the respectable classes of Bengal hence. And this will be affected without any effort to proselytize; without the smallest interference in religious liberty, merely by natural operation of knowledge and reflection".[16]

Macaulay's recommendation got the approval of Lord Bentick and it was published on the 7th March 1835. His forceful argument and usefulness of English language can be seen in his Minute, "The claims of our language is hardly necessary to recapitulate. It stands pre-eminent even among the languages of the west : it abounds with works of imagination not inferior to the noblest which Greece has bequeathed to us, with models of every species of eloquence, with historical compositions which considered merely as narratives have seldom been surpassed and which considere as vehicles of ethical and political instruction have never be equalled; nor is this all ! In India English is the langua spoken by higher class natives at the seats of government is likely to become the language of commerce throughout the seas of the East : it is the language of two great European Communities which are every year becoming more important and more closely connected with our Indian Empire—Whether we look at the intrinsic value of our literature or at the

14. The pp. 91-92.
15. *Ibid.*, p. 111.
16. *Ibid.*

particular situation in this country, we shall see the strongest reason to think that, of all foreign languages, the English tongue is the most useful to our native subjects".[17]

In 1835, government adopted Macaulay's scheme of modern education through English medium, but the teaching of English in a systematic way starts from the promulgation of Wood's Dispatch of 1854.[18] This Dispatch has been called the Magna Carta of Indian education. The Catholicity of its main recommendations is note-worthy *viz.* "*(i)* The constitution of a separate department for education; *(ii)* The institution of Universities at the Presidency towns; *(iii)* The establishment of institutions for training teachers for all classes schools; *(iv)* The maintenance of visiting Government colleges and high schools; and increase their number when necessary; *(v)* The establishment of new middle schools; *(vi)* Increased attention to vernacular schools, indigenous or other for elementary education and *(vii)* The introduction of a system of grants-in-aid". It was declared : "The English language is to be the medium of instruction in the higher branches, and the vernacular in the lower. English is to be taught where there is demand for it, but it is not to be substituted for the vernacular languages of the country. The system of grants-in-aid is to be based on the principle of perfect religious neutrality....."[19]

And, thus, new universities at the presidency towns of Bombay, Calcutta and Madras were established. The foundation of these universities marked a new epoch in the history of Indian education. Slowly but steadily, English medium schools and colleges increased in number and commanded more and more prestige. With the spread of schools and colleges, a very considerable number of Indians achieved mastery of English language and literature. The new education did not, as Macaulay had anticipated, revolutionize the structure of religious belief in India. Conversions were few and far between Hindus and Muslims took advantage of 'western' education but they remained Hindu and Muslims. Now the educated people of India would not tolerate any

---

17. *Ibid.*, p. 110.
18. *Ibid.*
19. *Report of Indian Education Commission*, 1883, pp. 22-23.

such move that would block the smooth progress of English education.

When the British government decided to withdraw state aid to Higher English education, people from all states reacted. Lord Curzon, who became the Viceroy of India in 1899 read these indications and could not overtake them. The proposal for the withdrawal of state aid was immediately quashed by his orders. He wanted to remove the chaotic condition of educational institutions. At the Simla Conference he discussed University education. He also dwelt upon secondary, primary and women's education, teachers' training and recruitment to higher posts in the Education Department. About what a university should be, he held a very clear idea and it is worth quoting : "It would be a place for the dissemination of knowledge and the encouragement of learning : and it further be a human smithy where character was forged in the furnace of experience, and beaten out on the anvil of truth".[20]

The English educated Indians now learned with growing success to speak in English, to write in English and even to think in English. But already the intelligentsia had become critical of the existing pattern of education. Such men began to talk of national education. They wanted a system of education in which the mother-tongue would be the medium of instruction. Their emphasis was on the use of the mother-tongue as the medium of instruction and on education closely related to Indian culture. On their demand, the government appointed the Calcutta University Commission in 1917. Dr. M.E. Sadler, Vice-Chancellor of the University of Leeds was the president of the commission. The Commission recognized the importance of the mother-tongue. They argued that mother-tongue may be used only in high schools; in the higher classes, they urged the retention of English. They said, "we are disposed to think that the educated classes in the various provinces of India will wish to be bilingual, to use their mother-tongue for dear and intimate things which from part of life from infancy upward and are the breath and substance of poetry and national feeling, to use English as a means of inter-

20. "A Collection of Lord Curzon's speeches on Indian problems", in *Lord Curzon in India Volume II*, pp.68-71.

communication necessary for the maintenance of the unity of India and a touch with other countries, for mutual exchange and stimulation of ideas in the sphere of scholarship and science and for the promotion of that international commerce and industry on which the economic future of India will largely depend".[21]

As English education was linked with Britishers, it was opposed by some great leaders who fought the struggle for freedom. Education aligned to national needs was advocated by Gokhale and others. Mahatma Gandhi who dominated the Indian political scene was against English education. He said, "The existing system of education is defective, apart from its association with an utterly unjust government in three most important matters : *(i)* It is based upon foreign culture to the almost entire exclusion of indigenous culture; *(ii)* It ignores the culture of the heart and the hand and confines itself simply to the head; and *(iii)* Real education is impossible through a foreign medium".[22]

Gandhiji was totally against English education. He gave a call to castigate everything that was English—language, manners, clothes—all. Therefore English education suffered a serious set-back. In his simple manners of writing, Gandhiji referred to the benefit effects of English education "....English is today studied because of its commercial and so called political values. Our boys think and rightly in the present circumstances, that without English they cannot get government services. Girls are taught English as a passport to marriage. I know husbands who are sorry that their wives cannot talk to them and their friends in English. I know families in which English is being made the mother-tongue. All these are for me signs of our slavery and degradation".[23]

But Gandhiji also appreciated the importance of a foreign language especially English. In his book *Young India*, he said, "I do not want my house to be walled in on all sides and my windows to be stuffed. I want the cultures of all the lands to be blown about my house as freely as possible. I would have

21. *Calcutta University Report Volume V*, p. 29.
22. Mahatma Gandhi, *Young India* (1919-22), p. 451.
23. *Ibid.*, p. 482.

our young men and young women with literary tastes to learn as much of English and other world languages as they like and expect them to give the benefits of their learning to India and to the world".[24]

By 1921, the mother-tongue came to be the medium of instruction in the middle schools and its use was extended to the high schools by 1937. The standard of teaching deteriorated due to frequent changes in the medium of instruction, changes in the aims and objectives of teaching in schools and colleges.

The Wood Abbot Report (1936-37) recommended an alternative in simplified English in order to keep the flow of education through the medium of English. But the estrangement with English was growing deeper and wider as the struggle for freedom gained more and more momentum. The Govt. of India Act (1935) was considered to be prelude to a proposed Dominion Status for India. On assuming office in 1937, the ministers busied themselves at once with educational schemes. In these schemes, vernaculars were the natural media of instruction. But at the secondary and university stages, English continued to dominate in the pre-autonomy days. All ventures of life, all avenues of success could be opened only with the keys of English. Thus the "position of English" in Indian educational system throughout the British rule was "enviable".[25]

Teaching of English : Post-Independence India

After Independence, a new epoch began amidst a horde of problems. It was in this context that English education and the use of English language were critically examined. Interesting discussions were forwarded in the Constituent Assembly proceedings[26] on the language issue. English was treated as a symbol of British dominance. English had to go, but there was no unanimity over the language which would

---

24. *Ibid.*, p. 484.
25. A.K. Sharma, *Aspects of English Language Teaching in India* (Bhagalpur : Bharat Book Depot, 1985), p. 31.
26. *Constituent Assembly Debates, Volume IX No. 32* (Monclay the 12th September 1949), pp. 1336-37 (The Constituent Assembly discussed the question of a national language from 12th September 1949 to 14th September 1949).

replace English. Therefore, English was allowed a lease of life under compulsion. In a changed atmosphere of the House, Sri Gopalaswami Ayyangar prefacing his resolution said, "we could not afford to give up English language at once. We had to keep the English language going for a number of years until Hindi could establish for itself a place that it can replace the English language".[27]

Almost all members felt that the medium of education should be one of Indian languages. In the words of the official language commission, "it can only be through the medium of Indian language that we should be able to bring about the massive resurgence of our national life in the service of the ordinary citizen which is implied in the adoption of adult franchise, free and compulsory education.[28] But almost all felt the importance of English language.

Agencies like the Central Advisory Board of Education, Inter University Board and the University Grants Commission were told to study people's attitude towards English and report. Honourable Maulana Abdul Kalam Azad was the first to suggest that Hindustani be heard from government branches instead of English. But he soon discovered there is no national language as such which can immediately take the place of English... "we have got to admit that so far as language is concerned North and South are two different parts. The union of North and South has been made possible only through the medium of English. If, today, we give up English then this linguistic relationship will case to exist".[29] When he was Education Minister, in his convocation address at Patna University, he said : "one thing is quite clear and definite and I am sure every Indian will agree with me. The position that English is occupying today in our educational and official life cannot be sustained in future. It is but essential that Indian languages should be given their legitimate position".[30]

But the Secondary Education Commission (1952) found

---

27. *Ibid.*, pp. 1318-1320.
28. *Report of the Official Language Commission,* Govt. of India, (1956), p. 33.
29. *Constituent Assembly Debates Vol. IX No. 32,* p. 1452.
30. Printed as an "After word" in M.R. Anand, *King Emperor's English* (Bombay : Hindi Kitabs Limited, 1948), p. 63.

that teaching of English should continue vigorously. The Commission recorded evidence to the effect that it was through a study of English language and literature that India became united and that she attained freedom. "Many eminent educationists and scientists have, therefore, expressed the opinion that under no circumstances should we sacrifice the many advantages that we have gained by the study of English. They hold that in matters pertaining to education sentiment should not be the ruling factor and that what was most urgently needed was that our youth acquire knowledge from all sources and contribute their share to its expansion and development. In the attainment of this objective, the study of English was bound to play an important part".[31]

It was true that English, in no way, should hold such a dominant position as it used to hold prior to independence but arguments for the claim of English to be retained in our educational system were strong and healthy. The regional language in place of English was not acceptable to many. Even Pandit Nehru, the then Prime Minister of India, took note of the linguistic situation and told the Conference of Chief Ministers in 1961, "The tendency of the regional language to become the media for university education, though desirable in many ways, may well lead to the isolation of such universities from the rest of India, unless there is a link in the shape of an all India language".[32]

The Secondary Education Commission was asked to collect information from foreign embassies in India about the position of English in their countries. The Commission found that in France, Japan, the Federal Republic of Germany, Egypt and U.S.S.R. English is taught as one of the compulsory foreign languages from school standard.[33]

But there were some leaders who opposed the retention of English. In the real spirit of agitators, they declared 29th January 1961 as Remove English Day. While the Castigators

---

31. *Report of the Secondary Education Commission* (Government of India, 1952), Chap. V, p. 64.
32. Reported in *The Sunday Statesman* (13th August 1961).
33. Report of *the Secondary Education Commission*, Government of India (1952), pp. 65-66.

of English were crusading without taking into account the other side of the case, the University Grants Commission took up the question of medium of instruction in 1959-60. The working group was composed of eminent Indian educationists and they were told to examine and suggest methods in order to bring about "an orderly change, whatever the change was necessary, consistently with the maintenance of standards".[34]

Three Language Formula

Hindi was to replace English for all practical purposes from 26th January 1965, as article 351 of the Constitution guaranteed. But imposition of Hindi was opposed by southern states. The working committee of the Indian National Congress studied the symptoms and then went into long deliberations. It found out a Conclusive formula of trilingualism which satisfied the prestige issue of all states. The fourth resolution of the Congress Committee on this issue is worth noting—"*(a)* national language of each state will become the medium of administration as well as instruction at the university stage as early as possible; *(b)* the standard of teaching Hindi will have to be raised; *(c)* English will continue to be taught as a language which has an important role".[35]

The recommendations of Kothari Commission (1964-66) were an epitome of wisdom and foresight. It made a comprehensive survey and examination of the entire field of education in a very short time. It laid emphasis on the importance of English. The Commission said, "while the goal is to adopt the regional languages, this does not involve the elimination of English which, as an important library language, plays a vital role in higher education. All teachers in higher education should be able to teach in the regional language and in English, and all students (especially post-graduates) should be able to follow lectures and use reading materials in English and in regional language... In major universities which draw their students from all over India, English should ordinarily be medium of education, though there should be freedom for Universities to experiment with the regional language as the

34. *Report on Medium of Instruction* (University Grants Commission, 1961), p. 1.
35. Reported in *The Statesman* (Calcutta : 3 June 1965).

medium of instruction. Special units for teaching English should be established in universities and colleges to impart a good working knowledge by adopting modern techniques".[36]

The government of India wanted to transform Indian education to make it more meaningful. The government wanted to relate it more closely to the life of the people through a three language formula. The Centre always impressed the state governments to vigorously implement "the three language formula which includes the study of a modern Indian language, preferably one of the southern languages, apart from Hindi and English in the Hindi speaking states, and, or Hindi along with regional language and English in the non-Hindi speaking states".[37]

Mrs. Gandhi, the then Prime Minister of India, also favoured three language formula. In her speech on 15th August 1967, she said, "It is feared that this proposal (for the mother tongue upto university level) might encourage separatism, and it can only be beneficial if there is a link language which can bind the people together. In the present day world, we cannot afford to live in isolation. Therefore there should be three languages, regional, national and international".[38]

All these efforts to see the position of English in India show that the question of discontinuing the use of English does no seem uppermost in the mind of the public. In fact, there has been increase in recent years in the demand for the study of English. This can well be understood by a recent development in the field of school education. A large number of English medium schools have been opened (in private sector) and people like to send their children to such schools. But the standard of English teaching kin schools and colleges has deteriorated fastly. The Ministry of Education and youth services urged the Study Group on Teaching of English (1971)[39]

---

36. *Commonwealth Universities Year Book* (Sydney Congress Year edition, 1968), pp. 1535-1536.
37. *National Policy of Education* (Ministry of Education, Government of India, 1968), p. 3.
38. *The Times* (16th August 1967).
39. *The Study of English in India* (Ministry of Education, Government of India, 1971), p. 3.

to prepare a practical programme for improving the teaching of English both at school and college.

The Importance of the English Language in India

It is true that English, in no way, should hold such a dominant place as it used to have prior to Independence. But arguments for the claim of English to be retained in our educational system are strong and convincing too. India needs a language of the outside world and English language stands relatively on a better position than any other foreign language like French, German, Chinese, Russian. Now the teaching of English as the compulsory second language is not challenged by any considerable number of people. Our late Prime Minister Mrs. Indira Gandhi often emphasized[40] the importance of English language teaching in our schools and colleges. She expressed her anxiety at the poor standard of its teaching.

English is the language of U.S.A. and other countries like United Kingdom, Irland, Rhodesia, New Zealand and Canada. It is taught as a second language in almost all the continental schools. It is understood and spoken nearly all over Europe and to a large extent in Egypt, Turkey, Iran, China and Japan. Dr. W.H. Gatherer has collected a very useful information regarding the teaching of English and its use in the world. "The modern world, however, is dominated by a few languages which are spoken by very large number of people : 350 million people speak Chinese, 300 million English, 160 million Hindi, 140 million Russian, 110 million Spanish. Though second to Chinese in the number of speakers undoubtedly the most widely spoken language in the world is English. Not only is it the first language of the United States, Canada, New Zealand, Ireland, Rhodesia and the United Kingdom, but it is the dominant language in South Africa, Nigeria, Kenya, India and many other countries. It is the preferred second language learned in vast majority of countries, only in one or two European countries being secondary to French and German. It has been estimated that 600 million people can use English competently".[41]

---

40. Reported in *The Indian Nation* (25 October 1983).
41. W.A. Gatherer, *A Study of English* (London : Heinemann Educational Books, 1980), p. 2.

The Knowledge of English, therefore, will enable us to establish intellectual, cultural, economic, commercial and political relations with the rest of the world. For higher legal, technical and scientific education and research in almost all branches of learning, its knowledge is essential. It is also necessary for those writers who wish to reach a bigger audience, for editors, lawyers, diplomats, politicians, in fact almost everyone.

The teaching of English in India, therefore, will continue as a second language where Hindi is the medium of education and as a third language where it is not. In learning two or three languages, we will not be a unique nation. To give up English would mean cutting ourselves off from the rest of the world. It is also a fact that the attitude of people is also changing towards learning this language. Gokak very aptly sums up the attitude of people as follows : "The English language has lined India with the world outside to India and from India to the world. We are blessed with the two way traffic that English has afforded us. We have paid a heavy price in the past for this privilege. But in our indignation over the price that has been paid, let us not throw away the privilege that is already ours. We may then have to condemn ourselves like Othello :

> Of one whose hand,
> like the base Indian, threw a pearl away
> Richer than all his tribe.

English is certainly not richer than our tribe. But it is a pearl all the same, and it would be foolish to throw it away".[42]

English, in India, has a definite place in the curriculum of Indian schools and universities. Our children will have to be bilingual and some of them trilingual. The learning of English will not entail any intellectual hardship on our students so long as it is the means of obtaining knowledge. But it is not meant to suggest that English and English alone can render benefits of enlightenment. When as many as 490 million Indians live in villages and they have to be given the share of the benefits of the developments taking shape within the country,

---

42. V.K. Gokak, *English in India : Its Present and Future* (Bombay : Asia Publishing House, 1964), pp. 178-79.

it is through vernacular alone that we can reach the masses and educate the whole of India.

The teaching of English in India as a second language or third language has been accepted. The teachers of English should better realise the need for and significance of English in the new perspective. They should revise their aims of teaching in the new setting. They should devise means to teach it most effectively within a short time. These are essential to achieve good standard of English. T.P. Reddi in his Presidential Address said in October 1977, "we, the teachers of English, are keenly alive to the responsibility that rests on us. We have to see that English is taught at all levels and taught well and its standards are properly maintained."[43]

The Problem of Declining Standards

The problem of declining standard of teaching English is not new. The very poor standard of English who want to be admitted in colleges has been admitted by Principal Barrow of Calcutta Presidency College in 1917. He told the Sadler Commission of Calcutta University: "When students come to College, they cannot follow lectures and they cannot read even quite simple English with ease. The curriculum is quite pretentious—Wordsworth, Milton, Arnold etc. This may not seem ambitious; but the fact is that students at the end of eight years are still without any command of modern English. Their vocabulary is extremely there. They know hardly anything of the idiom or rhythm of the language. In this condition, they are set to study 'literature' which depends for the success of its appeal on choice of allusions to the Bible, to European mythology and legend, and to English life and customs and history with which these boys are almost totally unfamiliar. (Their aim is to acquire) the bare literal meanings of words and phrases and allusions. To suppose that the reading of literature in this manner has any value whatever is absurd."[44]

The problem of declining standards was very much due

43. T.P. Reddi, "Presidential Address at the Third Annual Conference, English Language Teachers Association of India", *The Journal of English Language Teaching* (Madras : November-December 1977).
44. S. Nagarajan, "The Decline of English in India : A Historical Perspective," *College English*, 43/7, (November 1981), p. 663.

to aims of English education in general and English language teaching in particular. The aims were certainly very lofty and there were inadequate means to realise them. They syllabuses of English were literature oriented. The texts meant for Entrance, Under-graduate and Graduate Courses included masterpieces of Shakespeare, Milton, Goldsmit and poems and prose writings of Dryden, Pope, Blake, Bacon, Swift, Addison, Johnson, Southey and other great writers of English literature. The policy makers who prescribed textbooks for students forgot that English was not the mother-tongue of Indians.

The teachers of English also faced difficulties to solve the problems of students. They had to teach fundamental elements of language and the conceptual concept of the prescribed texts. The conceptual concept of the texts often had no similarities in the life of students. Therefore, the relied more on notebooks which were published in different parts of the country. Tej Bahadur Sapru and Professor S.G. Dunn at Allahabad before the Sadler Commission that notebooks had taken the place of original works of literature prescribed in the syllabus. Tej Bahadur Sapru told the Commission: "What is known as a critical study of any author really means nothing more than picking up a few telling sentences or striking phrases from some book of criticism without any real attempt at entering into the spirit of the author or appreciating his point of view".[45] Prof. Dunn also expressed the problem of the teacher in these terms : "The teacher found himself obliged to attempt two tasks at the same time—teach the basic elements of the language and also the advanced literary texts set in the syllabus. Since the two jobs existed at such widely different levels and since his own security of livelihood depended upon seeing the students safely through the examination somehow, the teacher of English settled down to become an examination coach, teaching the students how to arrive without travelling".[46]

After Independence, English Language teaching suffered a lot. It occupied a subsidiary place in the school curriculum. The number of periods developed per week were cut down

45. *Ibid.*, p. 665.
46. *Ibid.*, pp. 665-6.

and the number of years allotted to it in the course of secondary education. The result was a rapid decline in the level of attainment. At present the level of attainment of school students is pitiable. For this sad state of affairs, only students are not to be blamed, the present educational system is to be blamed too. The decline in the standard of teaching English may be ascribed, among other things, to lack of purpose and method, bad textbooks and unqualified teachers, faulty system of examination and inability to understand the true function of grammar and translation. The following excerpt from the report of a Study Group appointed by the Ministry of Education, Government of India, is a sad commentary on the predicament of English in India—"the standard of English is deteriorating very fast in our schools and colleges. In the country of Panini, the country that gave the science of Linguistics to the world, there were hardly any pupil in our regional medium schools who can write a correct sentence. If we speak of a group of sentences the statement can be extended with slight modification so as to include our colleges in spite of English being the medium of instruction and examination there. Scripts are assigned marks by University examiners not for what the examinees have said but what they meant to say. The English language has itself a ghost life in India. It lingers in on our examination scripts as a ghost like Plato's work of art. A vicious circle has established itself in these matters.....the younger lecturers being almost as incorrect in their use of English as the pupils themselves".[47]

India has been witnessing for sometime past a diminishing regard for English at the secondary and higher stages of education. V.V. John made a trenchant remark, "you could begin by accepting the fact that when most people discuss education, what they have in mind is how to get by without getting an education. When they discuss the language problem, what they are trying to decide is which language we shall be illiterate in".[48] Prof. Gokak has gathered some

47. *The Study of English in India* (Ministry of Education, Government of India, 1967), p. 8.
48. V.V. John, "The uses of English", Presidential Address at the All India English Teachers Conference (18th Anual Session), Chandigarh, December 29-31 (1967), p. 1.

amazing examples of the use of English language by students appearing at the S.S.L.C. examinations. They wrote, "Electricity is very use for one....Electricity was found many years ago. It is high position in the world", and students of M.A. final especialising in English language and literature wrote : "suspension is an important dramatic element. The Divine Comedy can not be said an epic. No plot is there believing upon which we can say that it is an epic" or a careless quotation, *viz.*

> "As wanton boys are to flies
> so are we to Gods".[49]

The deteriorating standard of English in India is very much clear from the above noted observations and quotations from Gokak. The only consolation that we can give to ourselves is the fact that it is a global phenomenon. Our neighbour Pakistan is also anxious over its deteriorating educational standards and it wants to improve the standard of English instruction. In a profile, Lawrence Ziring says "The sixth plan forecast greater attention to education and literacy....the country's deteriorating educational standards were not overlooked either, study of English language was given new importance and the government opened a drive to improve the quality of English instruction, arguing that there was a difference between studying the language and studying the English literature...The needs of science and worldwide communication made the study of English essential".[50]

Another statement which will be surely of interest to Indian teachers is to be found in the 8th report of Secondary School Examination Council of the Department of Education and Science in Great Britain. The authors of the report justified a change in the university entrance requirements. They said that the decisions of the Universities of Oxford and Cambridge to introduce a sixth form test in English language into their entrance requirements was based upon conclusion of their committees that "far too high a proportion of undergraduate

49. V.K Gokak, *op. cit.*, pp. 8-9.
50. Lawrence Ziring, "Pakistan's Military Rule : Problems, Prospects and Portents", in Asian Thought and Society : An International Review, Volume VIII, No. 24, (November 1983), p. 244.

at the time of their matriculation find undue difficult in expressing themselves accurately and clearly in their own language".[51] To these words of joint committee, the group representing Oxford University added "The standard of English appears to us to be in general regrettably low in the country as a whole".[52]

The Teaching of English in India : A Many-sided Problem

The teaching of English in India is a many-sided problem and the problems and their remedies will find adequate place in detail in the following chapters of this study. "In order to understand the full range of the problems of teaching English in India" says Dr. Awadhesh, "we will have to look at the question from other perspective as well. The three perspectives—the linguistic perspective, the learning perspective and the socio-linguistic perspective—in conjunction with each other will give a full view of what actually the problems of teaching English are. An awareness of the goal of teaching—what to teach, how to teach, whom to teach, and why to teach—is bound to ensure better teaching".[53]

The conditions of teaching English vary from state to state and even from place to place. By and large, the performance of the students in urban schools is better than their counterparts in rural schools. Likewise the attainment of the students in public schools or model schools is better than their counterparts in ordinary schools.

Some of the shortcomings in our programme of teaching English are lack of clear cut policy, little understanding of the aims of teaching English, dearth of competent teachers, wrong methods of teaching, defective textbooks, faulty examination system, insufficient provision of audio-visual aids, over-crowded classes, shortage of time and unsatisfactory supervision.

---

51. Report of Secondary School Examination Council on Examining of English Language (London, 1960), quoted in Albert H. Marck Ward, *Linguistics and the Teaching of English* (Bloomington, London : Indiana University Press, 1966), p. 11.
52. *Ibid.*, p. 2.
53. A.K. Sharma, *op. cit.*, p. 42.

Suggestions for Solving the Problems

It is needless to emphasize that in a developing country like India, the study of a foreign language like English offers vast opportunities. The policy regarding the place of English in our education system should be well defined. This should be determined keeping in view its use and vast opportunities in the field of science, technology, social sciences, philosophy, area studies, journalism, international trade and diplomacy".[54]

The teacher while teaching his students must keep in mind the aims of teaching English. These are *(i)* to enable the students to understand English when spoken, *(ii)* to enable him to write English, *(iii)* to enable him to speak English, *(iv)* to enable him to read English. He must know the standard of attainment to be reached in each class. Special efforts should be made to ensure that teachers of English themselves possess a good command of English. The school and college libraries should subscribe good journals which may enable them to know the latest developments in the field of linguistics and English Language Teaching. The teacher must be conversant with good methods of teaching. The examination in English need to be improved. Necessary audio-visual aids should be made available to schools and colleges.

The University Grants Commission should play active role in the development of foreign language discipline in the country. Research in the field of methodology, materials production, textbook writing and original research in English and foreign languages should be liberally financed.

The teachers of English are also expected to teach their students as effectivetly as they can. A summary of Prof. Nissim Ezekiel address to the teachers of English in India will not be out of place to quote, "without either hope or despair, I propose to discuss some basic attitudes at the grassroot level in the context of English teaching in India. The most widely prevalent may be labelled the mechanical as against the human. We have a job and we must do it. There is a prescribed text-book and a class room of students. Teach the former as best

54. Y.C. Bhatnagar, "Foreign Language Teaching in India : Problems and Prospects" in *Mainstream* (February 19, 1983), p. 20.

as you can....I suggest that the student would come alive and we would relate to them in their varied circumstances...As a small cross section of the teaching community at its annual conference, we are concerned only with the question of how to set our house in order and to what extent it can be done at present time....surely it is good for our profession to have persons in it who are well read, critically disposed and with a distinct sensibility regardless of the frustrations faced in the actual work on the job....We need a new impulse from the language, the literature and the culture which provide us with our livelihood".[55]

To sum up, we can say that English occupies a place of prestige in our country but at the same time we must accept that the standard of its teaching has deteriorated fastly and that is why it is essential to know the problems of teaching English in India. Then alone we can remove these problems and teach our students effectively for better results.

55. Prof. Nissim Ezekiel, Presidential Address at the 35th Session, AIETC, Pune, 1984.

2 Socio-political Problems of Teaching English

There is no denying the fact that the standards of English are fast declining in our country in general and in our state in particular. The reasons for this are too varied and complex. One cannot simply say it justifiably that teachers and their faulty methods of teaching alone are responsible for the deterioration in the standards of English in Bihar. We would like to raise certain socio-political and psychological issues which, we believe, are no less responsible for the falling standards of English in Bihar. John B. Pride, the well-known sociolinguist, has very aptly initiated a discussion on the sociolinguistic, political and psychological variables of English language learning in the Third World countries. He says,

> English in Third World countries characteristically possesses an ambivalent, even ambiguous character, relating uneasily with feelings of nationalism and of tolerance towards 'grassroot multilingualism' on the one hand, and with the not so 'blind desire' of common people to acquire the white man's language, on the other. Many different kinds of communicative need have to be satisfied, often in the same country, speech community, or family. Any comprehensive attempt to estimate the consequences the language learning would have to go far beyond the prevailingly psycholinguistic emphases of 'interlanguage' theorists, and would have to give greater recognition in particular to the transfer of communicative competences associated with native languages. There may well be motivated and sociolinguistically variable; the role of literature in non-native Englishes may be focal in this regard. Above all, it is time to place the study of language learning and using motivations on a proper bicultural and bilingual footing, so as to recognise the interplay of several

types of motivation with several type of linguistic repertoire.[1]

We will discuss here some of the non-linguistic factors which we believe both from observation and statistical evidence to influence success in English as a second language teaching. In the hope of presenting a reasonably clear picture of this complex domain, we will group these problems under three main categories, *i.e.* political, social and psychological.

The changing policies of the State Government with regard to the status of English in Bihar has contributed much to the deterioration of standards of the teaching of English and confused both teachers and students. In Bihar, the decision of the State Education Department to abolish the teaching of English in classes upto VII was given effect to in 1949. This experience of doing away with English made us fully realize the importance of English. The progress of university students who fell far short of the knowledge of English required at that level was extended in non-language subjects as well as in English. They also fared badly in services and careers where the knowledge of English was required. So a large section of the educated people of Bihar felt in 1959 the necessity of re-introducing the teaching of English in Classes VI and VII. The State Secondary Education Committee Report 1962 recommended that the teaching of English should begin from Class IV.[2] The State Government set up an Institute of English for training and retraining English teachers in 1962.

There was a great rush of admission seekers in English medium shools and no regional aspirations could stand in the way of self-interest of the guardians who had an eye for the inter-provincial and international career of their children. During the period 1958-65, the craze for English is apparent from the presence of a large number of private elementary and infant schools in the big towns of the state, even though these schools charged exorbitant fees. The importance was so

---

1. John B. Pride, " Communicative needs in the learning and use of English, " in *Indian Journal of Applied Linguistics,* Vol. IV, No. 2 (June 1978), p. 1 (Abstract).
2. *Report of the Bihar State Secondary Education Committee* (Government of Bihar, 1962, Para-15), p. 35.

much felt that the State Secondary Committee (1962) further recommended that " government secondary and multi-purpose schools at each divisional and district headquarters and the residential school at Netarhat should have parallel English classes by way of experiment".[3] Needless to say, the suggestion was not welcomed to and accepted by a considerable number of educationists of the State. It may be mentioned that a sizable section of the people of Bihar strongly supported those who launched " Akhil Bhartiya Angrezi Hatao Sammelan" which was first convened in January 1961 at Ujjain. This movement retarded the progress of English teaching in Bihar. The resolutions of the Sammelan are worth-nothing:

(a) not to cast their votes to people who use English in the Parliament or Assemblies;

(b) to urge upon the Courts of Law to act in persuance of Section 348 of the Indian Constitution and promulgate 'Hindi' or regional languages instead of English as the language of court business;

(c) to advise people not to transact deals with those shopkeepers who display their sign-boards in English;

(d) to impress upon the educational authorities to make the study of English optional, and substitute the same with an emphasis on the teaching of Hindi and regional languages, also making these the medium of instruction;

(e) to consider the students having failed in English only as having passed and suitable for promotion to the next higher class; and, finally,

(f) to urge the Government to introduce Hindi in the Army, Railways, Postal Departments, etc."[4]

The aforesaid resolutions had little or no impact on the teaching of English in other states of India, but it did much harm to the cause of teaching English in Bihar. After the general elections of 1967 in which the Indian National Congress

---

3. *Ibid.*, p. 35
4. Extract from the *Rapat: Akhil Bhartiya Angrezi Hatao Sammelan* (Ujjain, 1961), pp. 42-44 (Hindi version), quoted in S.P. Sinha, *English in India-A Historical Study with particular Reference to English Education in India* (Patna : Janaki Prakashan (1978), pp. 136-37.

was defeated in this state, a United Front Ministry was installed and there was no harmony between the Centre and our state on the lanugage issue. In the light of the above-mentioned resolutions taken by the activists of the 'All India Angrezi Hatao Sammelan' and on the populist demand made by certain sections of people of the state,the Bihar Government introduced a new provision to pass the matriculation examination. The Bihar government by a notification[5] made English an optional subject at Secondary stage. A provision was made that those students who passed in the aggregate and failed only in English would be declared 'pass without English'. This 'pass without English' provision was extended to Higher Secondary School students, too, by another notification dated 13th July , 1967.[6]

As it is very much true that what pleases the pupil is not always the right prescription; the decision of Bihar government regarding making English optional at Secondary and Higher secondary stages told upon the standard of the teaching of English in this state. The teachers as well as students were confused and the aims and objectives of teaching English in our state were lost. The standard of English fell to such an extent that students entering colleges were unable to write even a single sentence of correct English. Gokak's concern in this regard is relevant to quote:

> "You could begin by accepting the fact that even most people discuss education, what they have in mind is how to get by without getting an education when they discuss the language problem, what they are trying to decide is which language we shall be illiterate in".[7]

Again, in 1977, finding the importance of English language in the fields of higher education, technical education and vocational education and its continued deterioration in the standard of teaching in schools, the Government of Bihar decided to abolish the provision of 'pass without English'. A Notification[8] to this effect was issued on 10th January 1977. It

5. *Ibid.,* Appendix III.
6. *Ibid.,* Appendix III.
7. V.K. Gokak, *op. cit.,* pp. 8-9.
8. See Appendix III.

was decided that English would be compulsory subject at secondary and higher secondary stages and only such candidates would be declared successful who would pass in all the prescribed subjects of study, including English.

These constant vacillations between making English a Compulsory subject today and an optional subject tomorrow show that the Government of Bihar has not been steady in its policy regarding the place of English in the school and college curricula. It has been taking from time to time one step forward and two backward, and this callous attitude of the Government has kept all concerned in confusion. It is advisable, therefore, that the political and governmental interference in such educational matters as have far-reaching consequences on the future of the people of the State must end.

It is difficult to measure the non-linguistic factors which one considers likely to affect language teaching; however, we will discuss certain socio-psychological problems which influence the teaching of English in their own respective ways.

Lack of Motivation : In learning a second/foreign language as in other fields of human learning, motivation is the crucial force which determines whether a learner embarks on a task at all, how much energy he devotes to it, and how long he perseveres. It is a complex phenomenon and includes many components, such as, the individual's drive, need for achievement and success, curiosity, desire for stimulation and new experience, and so on. Besides these, there are two more aspects which are specifically important for second language learning situation, namely, communicative need and attitudes towards the second language community.

Lack of Communicative Need : The primary motive for learning a language is that it provides a means of communication. A person is, therefore, most likely to be drawn towards learning a second language if he perceives a clear communicative need for it. The extent of this communicative need depends upon the nature of the social community in which the person lives. In a multilingual community like India, for instance, the need for more than one language is apparent in a wide range of social situations. It is also reinforced by the cultural assumptions with which people grow up. A second language is, therefore, for many people, simply a normal and necessary extension of their communicative repertoire for coping with life's demands. English language in Bihar has no established functions inside the learner's community, but is used mainly for communicating with outsiders. The learners of English in Bihar, thus, are not constantly aware of a communicative need for it. For most of them, there is no such awareness at all. Many school and college learners of English in Bihar, for example, have no clear conception of themselves ever using the language for fulfilling real communicative needs, partly because they have little or no contact with the speakers of English and partly because Hindi serves their communicative purpose. English, however, provides an important means of communicating outside the boundaries of Hindi speaking areas where these learners perceive the communicative value of English and, as a consequence, are motivated to acquire proficiency in it. P.B. Pandit is of the view that Indians would be better off without being subjected to dominant languages such as Hindi and other local literary languages. "The region of northern India, where Hindi is the culture language also happens to be the region with the highest rate of illiteracy in the country". The notion of, dominant language is, after all, ' relatively new in the Indian situation, the more traditional picture has always been that of individuals commanding upto four or more languages, of which only one has been formally studied in school, and paying allegiance to no single dominant language. Language convergence ' at the colloquial level' is common in such cases, allowing for 'world to world translability' with no lack of communication across languages.[9]

We have so far made certain broad generalizations about the communicative need and its impact on the learning of English as a second language in Bihar. However, we have come across a large number of students in both schools and colleges, who appeared to be motivated by a sort of perceived communicative need. There is, thus, wide variation between the individual learners of English Bihar, as it is everywhere. The learners with a perceived communicative need reported

9. John B. Pride, *op. cit.*, pp. 2-3.

their innate desire for contact with the wider society, particularly with the English speech community. Many of them perceive a high degree of communicative value in English and reach an advanced level of proficiency in it. What is required is sincere effort to design courses to encourage all children to perceive English as a valuable instrument for communication.

Attitude towards the English Speech Community

When a earner is favourably disposed towards the speakers of the language he is learning, there are two main reasons why his motivation is likely to benefit. First, the learner with more favourable attitudes will wish for more intensive contact with the English speech community. In this respect, favourable attitudes reinforce the factors which make the learner perceive communicative needs. In situations such as ours, where circumstances do not actually compel us to have contact with the native speakers of English, the learner's attitudes may determine whether he perceives any communicative need at all. These two reasons concern mainly the purpose and nature of learning English as a second language respectively. There is a close link between the way we speak and the way we perceive our identity and our world. When we try to adopt new speech patterns, we are some extent giving up markers of our own identity in order to adopt those of another group. In some respects, too, we are accepting another culture's ways of perceiving the world. If we are agreeable to this process, it can enrich us and liberate us. If not, it can be a source of resentment and insecurity. One of the factors influencing how we experience the process is our attitude towards the foreign culture itself. If this attitude is negative, there may be strong interval barriers against learning, and if learning has to take place because of external compulsions, it may proceed only to the minimum level required by these external demands.

Ours is a learning situation where many learners have not had sufficient experience of the English speech community to have attitudes for or against it. In such situations, it is possible that attitudes relate more directly to learning as it is experienced in the class room. One important aspect of this experience is the image of the community which the learner derives from the teachers and the materials. If this image remains secondhand, however, it may remain a weak factor compared with more general aspects of motivation, such as enjoyment, stimulation through variety and, above all, the experience of success. It is significant that our study found no clear evidence that the learner's initial attitudes were important contributor to their eventual proficiency. However, successful learners were found to have developed favourable attitudes as the course progressd, and in their turn, these attitudes encouraged more success.

Looking at the problem from another angle, ours is a learning situation in which attitudes to the English speech community is less decisive in influencing motivation and proficiency, because here English is learnt primarily not for to sake of contact with the native speakers of English but for communication with those Indians who know English and have different mother-tongues. It may be pointed out here that English has increasingly taken on this function as an "international" language in recent decades, serving as a lingua franca either within a multi-lingual country, such as ours, or between people from different countries who do not speak each other's native language. Since we learn English primarily for this international function, we should not expect the learner's attitudes towards the English speech community to exert much influence. The motivation of the Bihari learners of English may, therefore, be called instrumental motivation, because they are interested in making English a useful instrument towards furthering other goals, such as gaining a necessary qualification or improving employment prospects.

Opportunities for Learning English in Bihar

A significant influence on the proficiency a learner of English achieves is the quality of the learning opportunities which the environment offers. Here, we will discuss four aspects of this influence: *(a)* the opportunities that exist for the use of English, *(b)* the emotional climate of the learning situations, *(c)* the type of language to which the learner is exposed ("his linguistic input"), and *(d)* the effects of formal instruction.

(a) Opportunities for Leaving English in Bihar: Language learning occurs through natural learning mechanisms which are activated when the learner is involved in communicative activity. If this is so, it is important that the learner should

have access to situations where the language is used as a natural means of communication. It is, however, sad to report that in Bihar, we have not so far created the communicative need for English and the opportunities for learning it through use. None of the students we interviewed, save those who study/have studed in English medium schools, do speak in English to their parents, brothers, sisters, classmates and teachers. We were astonished to learn that even in English classes, they communicate that even in English classes, they communicate with their teachers in Hindi or in their respective mother-tongues. Neither teachers nor English knowing parents talk to children in English. But for listening to their teachers speak English in English classes, students in Bihar have no exposure to the language. In majority of colleges and almost all Hindi medium schools, English, too, is taught through Hindi. It is only a microscopic minority of students who off and on participate in debates and discussions conducted through the medium of English. Essay-writing, elocution, recitation, mono-acting, drama and such other competitions and extra-curricular activities in English are conducted only in a handful of institutions and that too once in a while. Majority of students do not have radio sets in their houses, and those who have do not listen to the programmes conducted in English. Similar or even is the case with television. One of the greatest surprises was that none of those interviewed had ever visited English movies.

Under such circumstances, it is very difficult to create a proper English learning/teaching situation. Unless these barriers are removed, no improvement is possible in the field of English language teaching.

(b) Emotional Climate of Learning Situations : In an environment where learners feel anxious or insecure, there are likely to be psychological barriers to communication. Also, if anxiety rises above a certain level, it is an obstacle to the learning process. Unfortunately, the kind of situation where the learning of English takes place in the classroom, a situation where learners feel overanxious. In a typical language classroom, learners are often asked to perform in a state of ignorance and dependence which engenders feeling of helplessness. They are asked to produce unfamiliar sounds in

front of an audience. When they do not perform adequately, they are subjected to comment and correction, sometimes for reasons that are not clear to them. Majority of them do not possess the linguistic tools to express their own individuality. In any case, there is usually little opportunity for this, since the interaction is dominated by the teacher.

Similarly, a learning situation like ours may cause learners to feel anxious and constrained. With their limited communicative competence, they have difficulties in relating to others and presenting their own selves adequately. For example, making casual conversation or expressing spontaneous reactions becomes difficult, and attempts to do so result in misunderstandings and laborious efforts to explain. Unless they have firm confidence in themselves, they will come to feel that they project a silly, boring image, and become withdrawn . Their sense of alienation is increased by the fact that they are having to re-learn the conventions which surround simple daily events, such as eating in a restaurant or approaching an acquaintance. We have, however, come across some learners who do establish friendly contacts in the English learning environment which cushion their relationship with it and make them more willing to expose themselves in the new language. In the classroom, too, a sympathetic teacher and cooperative atmosphere do have a similarly supportive effect. It is significant that current discussions about methodology pay particular attention to creating such situations. We ought to keep it in our minds, however, that the level of anxiety felt by learners is only partly a result of the nature of the situation itself. It is also a result of personal factors. For instance, some learners have been seen being anxious more quickly than other, whatever the situation. Others have had experiences of failure which cause them to become anxious quickly in classroom learning situations.

We should also note that psychological research suggests that, at least in formal learning situations, we should not necessarily feel obliged to eliminate anxiety altogether. Whereas too much anxiety hinders learning, it seems that a certain amount of it can stimulate a learner to invest more energy in the task. However, the optional level depends on various factors, such as the learners' ability or the nature of the learning task.

(c) The Nature of the Linguistic Input : The nature of the kind of English addressed to the learners of the language is an important factor in influencing how well do they learn. It is now often proposed that the ideal input for learning English of a second language ought to be comprehensible, relevant to the learner's immediate interests, not too complex, but not strictly graded, either. Exposed to this kind of input, the learner's natural learning mechanisms are bound to operate, picking out the structures for which they are ready at any given time. The real problem, however, is that nobody has actually tested the effects of different kinds of input on learning English as a second language. Information about this would obviously be of crucial value for improving teaching. Most teaching approaches so far have been based on the assumption that the learner's input should be carefully controlled and graded for structural complexity. However, it is now sometimes suggested that this suggestion is mistaken, and that classroom should concentrate on providing the kind of input described above, that is, comprehensible, interesting, relevant, but not strictly graded. The curriculum planners and course designers must be careful in prescribing the teaching material for the students of English in the schools and colleges of Bihar.

(d) The Effects of Formal Instruction : It is true that in a situation where there is the right kind of natural exposure, formal instruction is not of much importance in learning English as a second language. In a situation like ours, however, formal instruction has got to be meticulous. In formal instruction, teachers attempt to affect the course of learning, mainly by such means as controlling the learner's exposure to the language, making them become aware of significant features and patterns, providing opportunities for practising the language, and ensuring that learners receive feedback about their performance. Within this general framework, an immense variety of teaching approaches is possible, and it is obvious that some teachers have developed more successful approaches than others. However, it is not very clear what factors determine their success.

There have been a number of studies comparing the effectiveness of different methods, such as grammar-translation or audio-lingual methods. These have been inconclusive, probably because no single method is intrinsically better than probaby because no single method is intrinsically better than others in all situations. Attempts to make fair comparisons are hindered by the fact that results are influenced by such a vast number of factors not related to the methods as such. These include the personality and skill of individual teachers, the ability and motivation of different learning groups, the availability of time and resources, and so on. In fact, one of the clearest conclusions to emerge is that at least in the present state of our knowledge about possible methods, these other factors together play a more significant role than the choice between one method and another. Besides, the effectiveness of specific techniques sheds light on pedagogical factors which do influence success for particular groups of learners, though such findings are suggestive rather than conclusive. We have found that the learners of English make better progress when they have teachers who use a lot of English in the classroom, do not rely too much on mechanical repetition, and provide visual stimuli. In case of college students, we have found that they learn better when practice with drills was preceded by an explanation of the structure involved. That formal instruction influences learning has also been substantiated by our ovservation that those who received more formal instruction are proficient in the language than those who received less of it. May be, it is so because learners of English in this part of the country do not have ample opportunity for natural acquisition through communicative use.

Ability to Learn

We have so far looked at two sets of factors which influence the success of a person in learning English as a second language, namely the nature of the person's 'motivation' to learn and the qualities of the 'opportunities' to learn. Now we turn to a third set of factors which make up the person's 'ability' to learn. We propose to use the term 'ability' in a broader sense than is often the case. The term is generally restricted to cognitive aspects of a person's ability to learn, notably intelligence and a set of more specific language learning abilities called 'language aptitude'. We use it here to refer to a broader set of factors which—given similar motivation and opportunities—make some people better at learning than others. We will use it to include not only cognitive factors, but also the effects of personality, age, and active strategies which the learner adopts.

(a) Cognitive Factors : There is a link between general intelligence and second language learning ability.[10] A school learner's average grades in all school subjects, for instance, are often a good means of predicting how good he would be at language learning.[11] It is also clear that success in learning English as a second language is related not only to general cognitive ability, but also to a more language specific set of learning abilities which are usually called 'language aptitude'. Language aptitude, maintain Carroll and Sapon, is a phenomenon whose exact nature is not yet known.[12] Intelligence and language aptitude have generally been found to correlate best with the more academic language skills which are often stressed at school, such as reading or performing in grammar-manipulation tests.[13] Attitudes and motivation, on the other hand, seem to be linked especially with the ability to use language for interpersonal communication. Another significant factor is the learner's strategies in categorising experience, for learners have to make suitable generalizations about the language.[14] There are some cognitive differences which dispose learners to particular kinds of learning and thus place them at an advantage, or disadvantage, in certain kinds of course. For example, some people seem to rely more than others on a visual stimulus, and might be more successful in a course where the written word is prominent. Another significant difference is whether a person is happier learning 'deductively' or ' inductively'.

---

10. See, R.C. Gardner and W. Lambert, *Attitudes and Motivation in Second Language Learning* (Rowley, Mass: Newbury House, 1972).
11. See, P. Mimsleur, *Language Aptitude Battery*.(New York: Harcourt Brace & World, 1968).
12. See, J.B. Carroll and S. Sapon, *Modern Language Aptitude Test* (New York : Psychological Corporation, 1959).
13. See, F. Genesee, " The Role of Intelligence in Second Language Learning", in *Language Learning*, Vol. 26, No. 2, pp. 267-80.
14. See, N.M. Naiman, M. Frohlieh and H.H. Stern, *The Good Language Learner* (Toronto: Ontario Institute for Studies in Education, 1978).

At the end, it seems reasonable to assume that learning English as a second language must be influenced by many other cognitive factors than those we have discussed here. Our knowledge in this area is still very limited and we must hope that future research will extend it.

(b) Personality : As with cognitive factors, a number of personality characteristics have been proposed as likely to influence second language learning.[15] These proposals are often supported by observation or intuition, but it has not proved easy to demonstrate them in empirical research. However, it is certain that personality will one day be shown to be an important influence on success in second language learning. The relationship, however, may not be a simple one. It is more likely that personality interacts in complex ways with other factors in order to affect learning. Other things equal, learners with high self-esteem are liable to achieve greater proficiency in learning the language.[16] Similarly, those who have greater tolerance for ambiguity score higher in tests of listening comprehension,[17] and those with a high capacity for empathy perform better in pronunciation.[18]

Age

For many people, it is almost axiomatic that children can learn a second language better than adults.[19] Language learning becomes an artificial laborious process after the ' critical period' during which the brain is flexible and language learning occurs naturally and easily. Since this period ends around puberty, adolescents and adult can no longer call upon these natural learning capacities. We, however, do not subscribe to this view. We agree to the view that children learn a language more quickly and easily than older people, but they do so because

---

15. See. G.R. Tucker, E. Hamayan and F.H. Genesee," Effective, Cognitive and Socail Factors in Second Language Acquisition", in *Canadian Modern Language Review*, Vol. 32, No. 3.
16. See,H.D.Brown, *Principles of Language Learning and Teaching*, (New Jersey: Prentice Hall, 1980).
17. See, N.M. Naiman *et al., op. cit.*
18. See, A.Z. Guiora *et al.*, " Language and Person, Studies in Language Behaviour", in *Language Learning*, Vol. 25, No. 1, pp. 43-61.
19. See, C. Qamsey and E. Wright, "Age and Second Language Learning", in *Journal of Social Psychology*, Vol. 94, pp. 115-21.

they have better learning conditions, more time, attention, communicative need, opportunities for use, and so on. Given similar opportunities to learners of different ages, adults are likely to learn more efficiently than children.[20] Indeed, the weight of evidence suggests that, given more or less equal opportunities, efficiency in learning a second language increases with age, and that younger learners are superior only in acquiring pronunciation skills.[21]

Whether a child, adolescent, or adult, what is required for smooth language learning is a favourable learning situation. The learners must be exposed to the language for long periods of time.

Active Learning Strategies

There are a number of active strategies which people might adopt in order to learn English more effectively. A successful language learner must employ a wide variety of strategies, demonstrating their active involvement in learning. They ought, for instance, to repeat silently to themselves the sounds they hear from the teacher or other sources of learning, such as radio, television, etc. They must participate sincerely in the activities of the classroom and take opportunities to discuss the lesson material with other students. Outside the classroom, they must exploit every opportunity to use the language as a means of communication, for example, by seeking personal contacts, listening to the radio/television or reading newspapers.

We have, thus, discussed here some of the factors which are responsible for the decline of the standards of the learning of English in Bihar. The problems of teaching English are not always the problems of learning English, for it is sometimes difficult to be certain how far the learning of English is the result of the teaching of English. Unless the socio-political and psychological problems are resolved, teaching of English in Bihar is not going to yield the desired result.

20. See, A. Fathman, " The Value of Morpheme Order Studies for Second Language Learning", *Working Papers in Bilingualism* (Toronto), No. 18, pp. 180-99.
21. See, C. Burstall, " Factors Affecting Foreign-Language Learning, A Consideration of Some Recent Findings", in *Language Teaching and Linguistics: Abstracts*, Vol. 8, No.1, pp. 5-25.

3 The Problems of Teaching English in School I and II

English is no longer the medium of instruction in our schools. It is as a second language that we learn/teach English in Indian schools. For children in the schools in Bihar, English is compulsory subject of study at Middle and Secondary stages. This is very much clear when we go through the chart procured by the Study Group, appointed by the Ministry of Education and submitted to the education Commission in 1965.[1] Hence, it is for the schools to rear up and supply sufficient number of young people with the kind of command of English necessary for communication with the outside world.

The teaching of English in Middle High Schools of our State is in shambles today. It has almost lost its relevance. The foremost task of school education is to enable the student to become moderately proficient in the use of language tools, but it has remained unfulfilled. English still holds a place of prestige in our country because if English is learnt well, it gives better prospects. Naturally, the guardians of school going children want to send their children to schools where English is taught well. The medium of higher education in quite a number of states is English, so a good foundation of English ensures a good higher education and a good prospect in getting a job. But the standard of the standard of the teaching of English in mother-tongue medium schools is not up to the mark.

Below are mentioned the broad structures of formal school education available in our State:

Primary Schools	I-V
Middle Schools	I-VIII
Middle Schools	VI-VIII

1. See, Appendix III.

Secondary Schools	VI-X
Higher Secondary Schools	VI-XII or IX-XII
Intermediate Colleges	XI-XII

Although it is a controversial matter when to start teaching a second/foreign language, the teaching of English in Schools of Bihar is started from class VI[2] when pupils are about 11 years of age. This age is the most appropriate stage where a child can learn a foreign /second language. W.F. Mackey's remark is notable in this context:

> In the introduction of a second language, practice in schools throughout the world varies from starting at the age of five to the age of fourteen. In some countries, national and social ideas prompt the early introduction of second language. In countries where the native language, has no recorded literature, a second language is introduced early enough in the primary school to permit the second language to be used as a medium of instruction. In most European countries, however, a second language has been introduced only after age of ten.[3]

Moreover , the learning of a language depends not so much on the number of years it is studied, but on the motivation of the students, the type of teachers, methods of teaching adopted and instructional material designed.

The standard of teaching English varies according to the type and the need of the school. There is no definite and set pattern of Primary and Middle education in the State. The elites send their children to privately managed schools which have classes from nursery to X or sometimes to XII. The teaching of English in these schools is certainly good. These schools have almost all the amenities, good teaching, attractive buildings, better management and devoted teachers.

The schools of the second category too, are privately managed, but the teaching of English there is not satisfactory. They have no amenities except that they are housed in a

---

2. *Syllabus for Middle/High School* (Education Department, Govt. of Bihar, 1979), P. VI.
3. W.F. Mackey, *Language Teaching Analysis* (London : Longmans, Green Company Ltd.,1966), p. 121.

comparatively good rented or self-owned houses and their teachers are generally unemployed graduates and post-graduates, who prefer earning 200/300 rupees sitting idle.

The schools of the third type are the Government Primary and Middle Schools managed by local bodies (Corporation, Municipality, District Board, Union Board, etc.) or the State Government directly. The schools of the first category are hardly a few in the State, the schools of the second category are mostly located in urban or semi-urban areas. The schools of the third category (government) are most common and they are located from big cities and industrial townships to remote villages. They teach upto class V or VIII. The total number of government Middle Schools is 11,805[4] in our State. These Middle Schools have a trained graduate Headmaster and five or seven matriculate trained teachers each. Some of these schools have their own buildings while others are in rented houses. Most of the rural and suburban population of the State and the poor of the urban areas send their children to these Government schools. In these schools not only the teaching of English, but teaching in general is in chaotic condition.

There is also not a definite and set pattern of secondary education in our State. About a decade back, there were a lot of private schools and the number of government schools was limited and they were situated at district headquarters of the State. They were called Zila Schools. The Headmasters of these schools were appointed by the Subordinate Education Service of the Government of Bihar. Teachers in these schools were appointed by the Director of Public Instructions. The private schools were run by governing bodies comprising local educationist, legislators, representatives of guardians and teachers, etc. The private schools had their own resources (fees and fines, donations, landed property) to develop upon. The government too gave annual grant as subsidy. On 2.10.1980, all private schools were provincialized and now no such private schools exist. Opening of private secondary schools has again been allowed by the State Government through an ordinance promulgated on 12.10.85.

---

4. *Report for the year 1984-85* (Education Dept., Government of Bihar), p. 9.

There are also some minority schools, run by Christian missionaries, Muslim Education Board, which do take financial assistance from the government, but the government has no control over their management. All these schools follow the courses of study framed by Bihar School Examination Board, Patna, which conducts the examination at the 10 stage. Some missionary schools having purely private management and schools in industrial areas are affiliated to either Indian Council of Education or the Kendriya Vidyalaya Sangathan, Delhi. The schools owned by the State Government come to about 90% of the total secondary schools in the State.

The standard of teaching in these Middle/ Secondary Schools has declined to a great extent and for this decline teachers, students, guardians, school surroundings, administrators, curricula, examination system, all are responsible.

English is introduced in class VI at Middle School stage. According to the present syllabus of English in Bihar, five periods a week are devoted to the teaching of this subject. Each period consists of 40 minutes. When the student passes Secondary School examination, he has already read English 3.20 minutes a week for five years. But the achievement of the student is a big zero in the present set up. Hardly a few students who have passed their matriculation examination can write a few lines of correct English. This wastage can be checked if we define the aims and objectives of teaching English in clear terms and then proceed with up-to-date, useful and scientific methods of teaching for realising these aims. In this sense, the various methods are related to various objectives. As such, the objectives should be stated and discussed in clear terms before we take up the material and methods of teaching English. The second language learning is not automatic. The child learns his mother-tongue and applies the habits of his first language to situations in the second. An Indian child is normally bilingual and learns the four skills of English at different stage of development. Therefore when the child learns a third language, both the languages earlier learnt come in his way. In the rural sector, speech as an objective of teaching English is unthinkable. He speaks simply to be able to read and gradually to understand. An urban child can develop his speech skill in his own interest to enable himself to communicate in his society and also to read and write. So the teacher has to think about these differences before he goes ahead to formulate the objectives. As Catford points out, "any language teaching operation takes place in a context of highly variable external factors, and must be adjusted to suit them", and he gives a list of some of them:

(a) the geographical situation, political affiliations and economic conditions of the country where the teaching is carried on;

(b) the eternal linguistic situation in that country (for example, is there one or more national language? Is the national language a 'world language' or a purely local language? Is there a large number of regional or minority languages? What uses are actually made of the particular L_2 we are interested in ?);

(c) the students' age, intelligence, educational and cultural background, motivation, etc.;

(d) the teacher's training, experience, cultural background, etc.;

(e) characteristics of language L_2;

(f) characteristics of L_1 and, especially, differences between L_1 and L_2.[5]

However, the objectives of any English teaching course are the development of four basic skills—listening, speaking, reading and writing to the best of pupil's ability. In the beginning of his learning the pupil should be occupied with the following pursuits:

1. The acquisition of an intelligible pronunciation.
2. The acquisition of guided and prompted talking.
3. The acquisition of a working vocabulary.
4. Practice in the reading of English.
5. Practice in transcribing and in simple writing.

According to Sharma, "During the first four years of

5. J.C. Catford, " The Teaching of English as a Foreign Language", in Randolph Quirk and A.H. Smith (eds.), *The Teaching of English* (London: Oxford University Press, 1964), pp. 141-2.

English teaching we should intend to develop in the learners the ability:

(a) to understand very simple English spoken at normal speed within the vocabulary and structures laid down in the syllabus;

(b) to speak very simple English with an internationally comprehensible pronunciation and intonation, as far as the environment permits, within the vocabulary and structures laid down in the syllabus;

(c) *(i)* to read aloud fluently within the vocabulary and structural range of the syllabus,

(ii) to read similar material silently with reasonable speed and to show evidence of comprehension by answering questions either in English or in the mother-tongue;

(d) to build simple sentences and paragraphs within the range of the syllabus without having to provide the ideas themselves.[6]

Now let us see what is taught in our schools to achieve these aims and objectives. As indicated earlier, English is introduced from class VI. Students have to go through only one book, namely *Learn English Book I* and structures 1 to 55[7] are expected to be covered. The distribution of marks is as follows:

1. Spoken English	15
2. Verse Speaking	10
3. Reading from the textbook	15
4. Handwriting	10
5. Simple dictation	15
6. Vocabulary	15
7. Structures	20
	100

In the second year of English, that is, class VII, *Learn English Book II* is prescribed and structures from 56-110 are expected to be covered. The distribution of marks is as follows :

6. A.K. Sharma, *op. cit.*, pp. 49-50.
7. Structures are quoted in Appendix II.

1.	Spoken English	10
2.	Recitation of poems	07
3.	Reading	10
4.	Vocabulary	20
5.	Structures	15
6.	Comprehension	15
7.	Handwriting	08
8.	Describing a picture/Answer to questions	15
		100

In the third year of English, that is, class VIII, *Learn English Book III* is prescribed and structures 111-165 are expected to be covered. The distribution of marks is as follows :

1.	Spoken English	10
2.	Recitation	05
3.	Reading	10
4.	Structure	20
5.	Vocabulary	10
6.	Comprehension	15
7.	Describing an experienced situation/ story telling picture composition/ paragraph writing /letter writing	30
		100

In the 4th and 5th years of English, that is, classes IX and X, only two books—*Learn English Book IV and Stories for Pleasant Reading* are prescribed and a new set of 48 structures is expected to be mastered by secondary school students. For grammar teaching the book entitled *A Current Grammar of English* is prescribed. In these two classes, there are two papers in English. Each paper is of 2½ hours duration in the final matriculation examination and carries 75 marks.

Paper I

The distribution of marks is as follows :

1.	No-detailed study	20
2.	Letter writing	10
3.	Paragraph writing	15
4.	Vocabulary	15
5.	Describing an event/Comprehension of unseen passage	15
		75

Paper II

The distribution of marks is as follows :

1.	Prose	30
2.	Poetry	30
3.	Grammar and Composition	15
		75

We find that the structural syllabus of English has been introduce in Middle and Schools of Bihar. It is based on the principle of vocabulary selection and control as well as the presentation of the structure patterns which English employs in order to convey meaning in a teaching order. In this approach, more emphasis is given on learning the basic sentence patterns than on learning the rules of grammar. The number of structure words in any language is limited and is rarely added to. Another assumption of the structural syllabus is that mastery over the signalling system of a language is more important than detailed knowledge.

But the basic question is whether there are a sufficient number of teachers to teach English according to the structural syllabus.? While teaching structural syllabus the use of mother tongue in the classroom should be minimum and this fact has been accepted by the authors of the books which are prescribed for the students of Middle and High Schools of Bihar . In a note to the teacher, the authors maintain:

> The structure used in the lesson should be presented orally first, in meaningful situations. They should also be drilled and practised with the help of substitution table. Speech is to be given priority. As the lessons are graded structurally, they should be taught in the right sequence and not abruptly. Vocabulary has been given as much attention as structures. The mother-tongue should not be used except in giving instruction and clearing a very difficult concept.[8]

8. Damodar Thakur, Bhuwan Ranjan and S.D. Sinha, *Learn English Book I* (Patna: The Bihar State Text Book Publishing Corporation Limited, 1981).

During our survey, we found out that most of the teachers, especially in the countryside, do not know the utility of structural approach to teaching English. They teach the prescribed books through the method of Grammar and Translation. It is because they have not been trained in the new methods and techniques. Thus, the first and foremost thing for efficient teaching of English is to find good and efficient teachers and retrain the existing teachers, making clear to them the usefulness of structural approach in the changed syllabus. In this regard , it would not be out of place to quote the following passage from Gatenby:

> Why is it that in all countries where a foreign language is taught a very large proportion of the pupils fail, after five or six years' work, to become proficient? The main reasons are: (1) unsuitable classroom conditions, (2) unsatisfactory textbooks, (3) wrong methods, and (4) untrained teachers. The last is the most important, for if we can train the teacher, make him efficient, and give him confidence, he can himself remove or gets round most of the other drawbacks. He can improve his classroom environment , and though he may not be able to reduce the size of a class, he will know how to get the best results from the fifty or sixty pupils he has to teach. As for the textbooks, the trained teacher becomes expert at making the best of even the worst specimen, avoiding its defects and adding what is necessary. And he is not likely to cause his pupils to suffer by trying to teach them by mistaken methods. It seems, therefore, that most of the obstacles to the acquirement of a second language will be removed if we can provide the perfect teacher.[9]

The teachers who are not trained should be immediately trained for better results. Before trying to teach any language, it is essential on the part of a language teacher to know the system of the language. This brings a teacher closer to the particular language structures. The knowledge of the word-order, the role of structure words, intonating, stress and rhythm is the first requisite of an English teacher. Comparing

9. E.V. Gatenby, " The Training of Language Teachers" in W.R. Lee (ed.), ELT Selections II (London: Oxford University Press, 1967), p. 213.

and contrasting the system of English language with that of the child's mother-tongue, a language teacher becomes well equipped in teaching his subject scientifically. The teacher of English should know what different methods and techniques are, what new procedures are being developed, what new instructional material is being devised and what testing devices are being evolved. The teacher should also know the reasons of a pupil's deficiency in learning the foreign language. It may be the product of a number of reasons: Psychological, social, economic and environmental. Unless the teacher understands the interplay of these forces, he cannot prove to be an efficient teacher. The English teacher should also possess adequate command over spoken and written English. His speech, including its pronunciation, stress, intonation speed and delivery, should provide imitable models for his pupils.

In Bihar, to improve the efficiency of English teachers, English Institute was established in 1962 at the State capital, Patna. This Institute now has been merged with the State Council of Educational Research and Training which was established in 1980. The Council has eight departments, and the Department of Languages is one of them. As said earlier, the main function of this Institute is to trained school teachers in the new technique of language teaching. Other important activities of the department are "instruction, revision evaluation, improvement of the language syllabus at the school level, organization of short and long term courses for language teachers and guidance in language teaching".[10] But this institute is not adequately staffed to carry on its responsibilities.

The foundation of competence in language is laid in schools, and thus it is very essential that teachers with good knowledge of English should teach school students. Untrained and inefficient teachers should not be given the opportunity to teach English. Teachers should be trained in such a way that they become capable of facing the new challenges in teaching English. As Gokak puts it :

> Untrained teachers are not competent to deal with this situation. Teachers who are trained are also generally

10. *Annual Report 1984* (The State Council of Educational Research and Training, Bihar, Patna), p. 12.

> unable to cope with it because of the doubtful utility of the training they receive in our training colleges. What is needed is something like a revolution in the methodology of English taught in our training colleges.[11]

In the first three years of teaching English in Bihar (*i.e.* from class VI to VIII), students are expected to learn how to read and recite poems and get proficiency in the use of 165 structures. They are also expected to write a paragraph on seeing a picture or, in other words they are asked to describe a picture. The books, *Learn English Books I to Book III* are to be taught to the students. These books are written according to the latest techniques of teaching English, therefore, teachers must know what is structural syllabus.

The structural syllabus is a list of linguistic items arranged in teaching order and accompanied by illustrative sentences. As language is primarily spoken, it should be presented in its spoken form first. Mastery over the signalling system of English language is more important than the detailed knowledge of the forms. This mastery is acquired by repetition or drill. The teacher's most important task is to create meaningful situations in the class. The principle of teaching one item at a time should be strictly followed, so that the pupils may acquire complete mastery over a given situation and may use it with full confidence in life situations. The items must be firmly established by plenty of oral work before the pupils read it in their books.

In the secondary schools (*i.e.* class IX and X) also, the structural syllabus is in vogue and teachers of English should keep the above-mentioned characteristics of the structural approach in mind. The pupil at the end of a 5 year-course is expected to know about 3,000 root words and their derivatives. He is also expected to master 213 basic structures of English.

In Schools, the time-table is divided into the teaching of reading, writing, composition translation and grammar and the teacher remains satisfied so long as his pupils are busy. It may be mentioned here that the Government of Bihar has issued instructions to its Middle and High School teachers regarding how and when to teach a particular teaching item

11. V.K. Gokak, *op. cit.*, p. 65.

prescribed in the syllabus. This monthly time-table for teaching is available with all schools-whether secondary or middle but no teacher was found doing his duty according to the time table.

As the teachers of English in India are often ignorant of the objectives of teaching English as a second language, those teaching English in our State, too, are no exception. They resort to methods which are not based on recognized principles. In schools, teachers of English are seen sitting idle for the whole period. They ask one of their pupils to read aloud a part of the lesson and other students of the class with their books open to listen to him. Each boy gets his turn and the period ends. Undue emphasis is laid on oral work and too little attention is paid to drill in the elements of language. Owing to this defect in the teaching of English, teachers' efforts, if any, prove ineffective. In order to remove this defect, an adequate number of dedicated teachers are a must and they should know what actually a good method of teaching English is. What Faucett said long ago about a true method of teaching is still relevant :

> A true method should be comprehensive—that is, it ought to take cognizance of all branches of English that may be taught; it should be sound-based upon accepted principle; it should be elastic/ adaptable to the varying conditions in which it may be applied.[12]

As the syllabuses of English in schools are structural, the method of teaching should also be structural. The Grammar Translation method, does not fulfill the purpose of teaching English syllabuses. The direct method needs rationalization since English is a second language. It requires modifications in order to be an effective tool of teaching the language. The approach to the language through structures arose out of this need. In order to learn the language and various skills of the language, one should know its structures, handle them in various situations and master them for the purpose of various skills. The success of the scheme rests on the fulfilment of certain basic conditions. There should be ample oral work

12. Lawrence Faucett, *The Teaching of English in the Far East* (Harrap, 1938), p. 19.

through repeated practice and drill to establish a structure in the mental make up of the pupils. Pupils should acquire the ability to speak English as soon as possible, as oral work is a very important part of the syllabus. Teaching of English in the schools should be started in the very beginning, because "oral practice is the quickest way of getting started. Speaking is quicker than reading or writing.... To be able to speak a language makes that language more living and real to a child than to be able to read or write it".[13] And the conditions in India warrant the adoption of the structural way of teaching in view of the changed objectives of teaching English. The role of the secondary schools is limited to the development of the basic skills of the language with the graded language material in the shortest possible period. If it is to be achieved the way the language should be taught in schools must be planned. The structural approach gives us that plan. But we should always remember that the implementation of the approach through appropriate method and technique depends upon the quality of the teachers, their command over the language, their understanding of the structures, their mastery over them, their training and their professional qualities and character.

One of the notable problems of teaching English in Bihar is the problem of numbers. There has been an ever-increasing rush for education during the last forty years and on account of this classes have become overcrowded. The urge for education has been growing among the masses, bringing more pressure on schools which have shortage of buildings, funds and experienced teachers. The increasing number in the classroom is bound to affect teaching of English. Language learning is a skill to be drilled. It is not mere information to be given. That is why proper teaching is not possible in an overcrowded class. It is also fact that extreme variation is found in the quality of students studying in secondary schools. As there is no state level examination before class X, a well-defined yard stick for promoting students to the next higher class does not exit Consequently, many students reading in

---

13. H.G. Wyatt, *The Teaching of English in India* (London: Clarendon Press, 1950), p. 19.

classes from VIII to X do not know the basic things that an average student of class V or VI is supposed to know. The main problem with such students is to teach them their own language with correctness and precision because they never hear their own language spoken correctly at home. When these children are required to be taught correct speech in their own language, they are left with very little energy to devote to learning a second language like English, which is basically different in structure and sound from their mother-tongues. English under these circumstances definitely hinders their progress in school. Therefore, such students need special care by their guardians and teachers alike.

As English is chronologically speaking a third language in school curriculum in Bihar, for its successful teaching, daily lesson planning is essential, but it is not practised in most of the schools of Bihar. Daily lesson planning is as essential as planning the general courses. When the course has been carefully planned, many important aspects of lesson planning already have been anticipated. Specific lesson planning is, therefore, dependent upon good course planning. The teacher has to keep clearly in perspective the total learning contemplated in the course. Then alone will each day's lesson contribute towards the achievement of the objectives of the course. The idea of Bossing about what is a good lesson planning is worth noting:

> Lesson planning is essentially an experience in anticipatory teaching. It is living through in advance, mentally and emotionally, the class-room experience as the teacher visualizes it. The eager faces, the question that will arise, the difficulties the pupil will encounter the way these difficulties are to be met—all these will the teacher experience in imagination. This is the first essential of good teaching.[14]

Our teachers of English do not value the importance of lesson planning because they are not properly trained in training colleges. Needless to say, most of the teachers of English in our middle schools have got no training at all either

14. Nelson L. Bossing, *Teaching in Secondary Schools* (New York: Amerind Publishing Co. Pvt. Ltd., 1970), p. 184.

at the Institute of English, Patna or at Training Colleges, because most of them are matric-trained. This training programme is given to those candidates whose qualification is just matriculation and they are admitted to Primary Teachers' Training Colleges where English method is an extra paper and only a few students offer this subject. They need, therefore, to be retrained in the current methods of teaching English.

The lessons of English should be prepared in such a way as can have the quality of internal consistency, logical development and can leave possibilities of interlinking themselves with the preceding as well as succeeding lessons. Children must have the feeling that there is definite joy and gain in each lesson. In this way, we can prepare lessons in English as comprehension lesson, grammar lesson, lesson on composition or on poetry. If it is a lesson on structural situation, the teacher has first to look for the main structural point. He has to teach those first; he prepares a few new sentences which should clearly reinforce the learning of the structural point. Very close to the treatment of structural items comes the need to introduce vocabulary. He moves back and forth between presentation and pupil practice of individual and group drills of various type. The treatment of structural point should precede the treatment of theme or ideas so as to facilitate the understanding of the language. In school syllabus, the aforesaid approach is practicable right through the middle grades to class X. In every class, the teacher is likely to meet a few weak students. They should be assisted . The intelligent ones should be given opportunities to lead groups in dialogues, in drawing and sketching, in arranging activities.

The low standard of the teaching of English in our schools is also due to the lack of necessary facilities. It goes without saying that the teacher is favourably affected by good environment condition. When students approach their work with pleasure, the teacher cannot but feel a buoyancy of spirit and satisfaction in his work, not otherwise possible. Six or seven hours in schoolrooms under unhygienic conditions are likely to affect seriously the teaching and health of students. Let the matter of unhealthy atmosphere of schools lay aside, but teaching aids cannot be overlooked. Without necessary teaching aids, a teacher is not expected to do his work efficiently. In some of the middle schools of Bihar, we do not even have in adequate quantity decent blackboards, erasers and chalk. Some of our larger schools situated in towns are fortunate in this regard . Many desirable things may be lacking, but basic facilities they must enjoy.

Blackboards have been considered indispensable to the school and so they really are. An extensive library is more and more becoming a necessity of a good school. In countryside schools, there is no library. Many educators rightly consider a large working library as the very heart of the modern school's equipment. In this regard what K. Bose feels is very appropriate:

> Our rural school atmosphere defeats the very purpose of suggesting the maintenance of a desirable condition or standard of teaching English. Right from the teacher preparation and placement to the actual teaching of English that goes on in a rural school, one can experience a sad spectacle around a vain effort and that is ' teaching English'. It is the whole chain of thought that comes back to the mind that constantly does remind one, "they better not learn English".[15]

It is heartening to learn that the Government of Bihar has decided to equip most of the schools with radio and television sets. Possibly, no single achievement within this generation holds more actual and potential significance for education than the development of television. Every school can, through the radio and television, greatly enrich its existing programmes. It may be noted that Central Institute of English and Foreign Languages, Hyderabad has been doing excellent job in promoting the teaching of English in India. The Annual Report (1983-84) lauds the role of CIEFL, Hyderabad in these terms:

> The Institute has done pioneering work in the use of mass for the teaching of English. A five year integrated course, in English, in the form of radio-programmes, prepared by the Institute is being broadcast by 25 stations of all India Radio. A programme meant for the teachers of English is

15. K. Bose: *Teaching of English : A Modern Approach* (Delhi: Doaba House, 1979), p. 250.

also being broadcast over AIR. The Institute has also prepared T.V, programmes on an experimental basis. Preparation of Radio/T.V. programmes also forms part of the training courses at the Institute. Under the U.G.C. scheme of Educational Media Research Centres, one such Centre is being set up at this Institute. This Centre will be producing educational programmes to be telecast using INSAT-B and will serve the needs of other educational centres in Hyderabad.[16]

It is hardly necessary to emphasize that such broadcasts should be handled properly and students should be given opportunity to hear and teachers themselves will be benefited by listening to these programmes of the All India Radio. This will improve their pronunciation of English. So far as the Classroom visual aids are concerned, they are many like photographs, art picture, lantern slides, film slides, motion pictures, television, etc; semi-pictorial devices like maps, charts, diagrams, graphs, blackboards; objects like globes, models, specimens. Unless the teacher uses wisdom in the selection of concrete material, excessive waste of pupil-teacher energy will result and school will become involved in unnecessary costs of questionable materials.

So far as the examination in English at school level in Bihar is concerned, it dominates the scene and it seems that passing the examination is the only end in view. Now the examination which is conducted by Bihar School Examination Board has lost its sanctity. B.S.E. Board conducts the school leaving examination of those students who have read up to X. In this examination, large scale of bunglings take place. Transaction of thousand of rupees occurs between the board and the school authorities in the selection of schools as examination centres. This is all to earn easy money. These schools then earn money more than what they spend by favouring the examinees by allowing them to use unfair means, mass copying and impersonation. In this sad state of affairs, the teaching of any subject is not possible. It is not that the government is unaware of the fact but either it is helpless or it

16. *Annual Report (1983-84)* (Ministry of Education and Culture, Government of India), p. 77.

has no will power to check the malpractice being done by a host of officials, headmasters, teacher-invigilators, members of flying squads, observers, etc. These things tell upon the future of bright students who lose all their enthusiasm to labour and achieve something in their life when their friends pass with good marks without any labour. By virtue of mass scale of unfair means the proportion of successful candidates at the matriculation examination of 1985 was 80% of the total candidates appeared. The figure amply reflects the quality of students going for higher education at colleges or also to be admitted in the Primary Teachers Training Colleges meant for producing teachers for primary schools. Thus we see that the standard of examination at secondary stage is deteriorating fast and so far as evaluation of answer books of matriculation examination is concerned, it is also not fair. On many occasions, teachers become examiners in subjects they never studied or taught or had any contact. Under such circumstances, their mode of marking is average and naturally they do not do justice with the job entrusted to them. These are really grave dangers which can eat the very fabric of education and under such circumstances, teaching and learning a second language become very difficult.

Now let us think what can be done to improve the standard of teaching of English in the exiting situation. From the first year of teaching English to the third, much emphasis is to be given on the spoken English. It is really regrettable that in most of the schools, its importance is not being understood. For improving the speech of students, two things are required. Firstly, they must listen to correct and effective speech of someone who speaks English reasonably well. Secondly, they should try to speak in the same manner to enable themselves to speak. Therefore, a teacher should, first of all, acquire correct pronunciation himself and then try to present English sounds in meaningful sequences—in words and sentences in a bid to impress upon the learners to listen to them accurately and render them correctly too. He should also give practice in patterns through varied situational drills, pay special attention to those features of English pronunciation, which are interfered with by vernacular pronunciation or which do not exist in the vernacular. He should attempt to correct errors in speech through speech drills, games , songs and recitation.

The teachers of English should remember that practice in speaking at the early stage of learning facilitates language learning. However, practice in the early stage of learning should be limited to sounds vocabulary or structural patterns which are being taught for active production. The students directly after the imitation and repetition exercise face difficulty and frustration. They obtain a limited number of language contacts in their imitation drills. Then, they require a sort of stimulus to speak something in English, for want of which when they are asked to describe a room or house, a railway station, a shop, etc., they have normally considerable difficulty to do so even in their mother-tongues, not to speak of English. Some ways and means must be devised to supply the pupil constantly with ideas on one hand and language items on the other. Use of pictures can be helpful in this regard. When pupils have made sufficient progress in speech exercises, the teacher should help them in arranging facts and expressing themselves in continuous speech.

The next important item in the English syllabus for the beginners is reading. As reading is the best auxiliary to the teaching of composition, children should acquire at an early age a taste for reading. The teacher should choose two or three words out of the vocabulary built through oral work. He should point to each word, pronounce it, and finally ask the pupil to read the words from the blackboard. Then he should analyse the words into component letters, thus enabling the pupil to grasp the spelling. After practice with words, the teacher should write the sentences learnt in oral lessons on the black board, and ask the pupils to read them. Sometimes, pupils themselves may be asked to write words and sentences on the blackboard.

The students should be introduced to text-books only after a considerable practice in reading from the blackboard is done. For the first few years, it is better to deal with familiar Indian life and to exclude distinctly English life and English illustrations. English topics should, therefore, be introduced only when the child has become familiar with his domestic and school vocabulary. Equal attention should be paid to the language in which the material is presented. Words and phrases should be graded according to difficulty. Bihar State Text-Book Publishing Corporation has published all the books prescribed in school syllabus for English and it must be acknowledge that much care has been taken in this regard.

When the student reaches class X, he has to go through a book, *Stories for Pleasant Reading*, which is prescribed for no-detailed or extensive reading is also essential, for majority of students remain shut our from the world of books throughout their lives and find no joy, no mystery, no message in reading the prescribed text-books. Extensive reading is also essential for enriching and refining the minds of students. We should, however, keep it in our minds that the purpose of extensive reading, too, is primarily linguistic. We have to enable the pupil to use English as an ordinary channel of communication.

The skill of writing also occupies an important place in the teaching of English as a second language. In teaching English, the teacher aims at developing four abilities: ability to understand, to speak, to read and to write. The teachers of English should pay full attention to written work which is in no way less important than reading and speaking. Educationally, the learning of language is not complete, unless its graphic skill is acquired to a satisfactory level. The first and foremost requirement of good writing is a good handwriting. The qualities of a good handwriting may be listed thus:

(i) It should be legible. A bad handwriting is a sign of an untidy and confused mind.

(ii) A good handwriting also means writing with good speed. The teacher, however, should take more care of legibility than speed.

(iii) It should be attractive.

The next thing that the teachers of English must take care of is the spelling. Errors of spelling are strewn all over the written exercises of our students. This is because English spelling presents difficulties to the foreign learners owing to its irregularities and eccentricities. Our students are confused because their vernaculars are phonetic, in which each letter stands for an articulated sound. They can be taught by the two well-thought methods of teaching spelling, *viz*., the incidental method and the drill method. In the incidental method, no separate period is set apart for drill in spelling, and students are not asked to memorize lists of words. The teacher draws the attention of his student to the correct spelling of words in the reading and other lessons. The incidental method, however, ought to be supplemented by some kind of drill.

In the second year of English teaching, student should be asked to describe pictures, for pictures afford a vital motivating force to the pupils of English in making them bring their passive language to the level of active expression. Pictures present a vivid situation, especially coloured pictures help the pupils recognize the living details of a situation and find our appropriate language material for expressional purposes. Schools should, therefore, provide a large variety of pictures dealing with different aspects of social life.

In the third, fourth and fifth years of teaching English, pupils are expected to write letters, paragraphs, etc. Paragraph writing is a kind of free expression and it can be taught to pupils of all classes. The beginners may get a descriptive subject related to persons and places taken from school life. The next higher group may be given topics from social life surrounding them. The top classes should get topics of general interest which should acquire an element of comment or discussion. They may be told to write letters because letters are the simplest and most spontaneous form of written composition.

In secondary classes, we have to teach both prose and poetry. The poems prescribed are simple in diction and content too. The major themes dealt with in the poems are simple human relationships, natural sights on season etc. Most of these poems are from John Bunyan, Charles Mackay, William Wordsworth, Thomas, Hood and Robert Herrick.

The purpose of teaching poetry to Secondary School students is to enable them to understand and appreciate the poet's style and imagination, to understand the subtle thoughts conveyed by the poet, to enjoy a poem, its poetic beauties and to develop a taste and love for poetry.

The purpose of teaching prose is to enable them to increase their knowledge of both the language and the subject matter, or to enrich their intellect.

While teaching a poem, the teacher should read the poem aloud once or twice. It is desirable that the teacher should expose the most outstanding feature of the poem he is going to teach. Suggestive questioning can lead to the understanding of the since. At last, a discussion can follow. Students should be encouraged to give their own interpretation of the poem. But, at the same time, teachers should keep this in mind that how a poem should be taught depends more on the teacher.

So far as teaching of English Grammar is concerned, it is sad to report that in some schools only little grammar is taught. The English syllabus prescribed for school students includes a substantial portion of formal grammar with a view to strengthening the language skills of the learner, but the formal grammar has to wait for three years, because in schools of Bihar, the structural syllabus is drawn up in such a manner that for three classes *i.e.*, VI, VII and VIII, grammatical elements are found integrated in the structures taught. The books present the content in the form of either ' Sentence patterns', such as Ram gave Shyam a book (N+V+direct obj.) or teaching points, such as, ' There is a pen (Introductory 'there') or, the pen is on the table' (Preposition, 'on'). The teacher is supposed to teach the teaching points, thus structured for three years without ever feeling the need of bringing in or explaining the 'formal' grammar terminologies.

From Class IX, *i.e.* the fourth year of teaching English, a course in formal grammar is introduced. This grammar course very much resembles the traditional grammar. For example, pupils have to learn parts of speech, form classes, direct and indirect narration, transformations, punctuation, syntax, time and tense relationship, etc. Besides formal grammar, students have also forty-eight structures to learn. The textbooks of English meant for Classes IX and X are designed to give exhaustive practice in linguistic elements and patterns.

The teacher of English is expected to give proper drill of patterns prescribed in the syllabus for better results. He should contextualize the patterns in the lessons of the textbook.

There is evidently a plan to keep the grammatical elements very close to their application in the text. This way the purpose of teaching grammar will be fulfilled. The pupils at the school stage are too full of life and vigour to be crampt into the formal approach of grammar. They would like to feel the language, experience it and breath it. The function of the teacher is to see that his pupils become interested in the language and develop a positive sensitivity to it rather than equip them with a bag of definitions. It is necessary to build up the linguistic attitude in the pupils.

The teacher of English should also keep in mind the fact that English grammar has been completely recast on a new model. For example, ' qualifier' is a term used for words, phrases and clauses which qualify nouns pronouns, adjectives, adverbs and verbs. Previously, in the traditional grammar, the word modifier was used. The various noun qualifiers or pronoun qualifiers constitute the class, known as 'determiner'. The determiners are: the, this, that, these, any no, some what which , whatever , whose, whichever, both, all, a, an, each, either, one, my, your, his, her, its, our, their.[17] In the traditional terminology, we were familiar with the term called 'article' and then would include only 'a'/'an' and 'the' as articles. The list presented above shows how the function of different elements in Syntax is constantly being reviewed. The teachers of English must, therefore, consult authoritative documents on Modern English Grammar.

The standard of teaching English in schools can be maintained if we teach this subject properly. The air of teaching English to school students is to enable them to make simple sentences, to express their ideas with proper stress and intonation. They are expected to write legibly and speak short conversational sentences. They should be able to read the material appropriate to the level, and should be able to use newly learnt words. For three years of teaching English, formal grammar should not be taught, but their vocabulary should be of about 1000 words. This we can achieve by adopting appropriate methods of teaching. Method means selection

---

17. L.A. Hill : *A Guide to Correct English* (London : Oxford University Press, 1965), p. 204.

gradation presentation and repetition of the matter in an effective way. At secondary stage, we should try to raise the level of the language and literature already learnt by our pupils. If there are some misconceptions in the minds of teachers regarding the teaching of English, these misconceptions must be removed. Some teachers and headmasters think that too much of attention to the teaching of English is tantamount to inadequate attention to Hindi and other school subjects. But this belief has no basis and it needs no clarification. It is a fact that we do not have sufficient and competent hands to teach English, but the existing staff should leave no stone unturned in teaching the subject. If there is a sense of dedication among the teachers, they can themselves be able to resolve the problems faced by them in the day-to-day teaching of the subject.

4 The Problems of Teaching English in Colleges and Universities

The teaching of English in colleges and universities of Bihar presents a very gloomy picture. Although there has been a remarkable progress in the field of higher education after Independence, yet there has been a degeneration in the quality in proportion to the quantitative progress in higher education. Till 1950-51, there was only a single university, the University of Patna in Bihar, but at present there are six general universities, namely Patna University, Bihar University, Bhagalpur University, Magadh University, Ranchi University and L.N. Mithila University, one Sanskrit University and two Agriculture Universities.

The problems of teaching English are the problems of teaching in general. The marked deterioration in the standard of teaching English, however, has created a number of problems in our educational life and thought. The students of Bihar after passing from our colleges find themselves at a loss when they are asked to write a few lines of English. Let the matter of English be laid aside, they cannot even express or write correctly in Hindi. It is seen that students of Bihar, who go to Delhi or to other important centres of learning, do much better in all India competitions than those who study in Bihar itself. This phenomenon is indicative of the fact that there is something wrong with the system of higher education in Bihar. One of the major reasons for the poor performance of our students at national level seems to be their poor capacity to express themselves in English with fluency and ease. This aspect, therefore, needs special attention.

Some people denounce the present education system itself forgetting that it is this very system which has produced a large number of eminent personalities. It is true that the prevailing condition in our educational institutions, especially universities, is quite distressing. Teaching is the worst casualty. In most places teachers do not give full attention to the teaching work assigned to them and run after private tuitions. Making money seems to be their *summum bonum*. The students are not getting from the teachers what they deserve and in consequence they want to pass examinations by adopting various kinds of unfair means. Many teachers have lost their reputation of being fair and honest examiners. The fast deteriorating conditions prevailing in the educational world—its administration, teaching, examination, discipline—have been harming all concerned.

The higher education in Bihar is stratified into:

(i) Intermediate Colleges (+2)

(ii) Degree Colleges (+3)

(iii) Post-graduate Colleges and Departments

Intermediate education till 1980 was imparted exclusively in the degree colleges and its examination was conducted by the respective universities. In February, 1980, however, the State Government established the Bihar Intermediate Education Council to direct, supervise and control the Intermediate education in the State. This Council failed miserably in the discharge of its duties and was abolished in May,1985. Now the government thinks of delinking Intermediate education from degree colleges. The Collegiate education in the State has received a major setback with the introduction of a new ten plus two plus three (10+2+3) pattern of education. But this decision is being implemented in keeping with the national policy of education. Of late, higher education in Bihar has lost its sense of purpose. The credibility of educational system has been threatened by frequent irrelevant changes in the government policy and meaningless experimentation in the field of higher education. Hardly a system attains maturity when it is replaced by another adding to the confusion of the academicians. With changes of governments, the whole educational system is changed and consequently stability eludes the institutions of higher learning in the State. It is remarkable that no worthwhile step has been taken up by any government to streamline teaching and examination—the fundamentals of higher education.

At present (+2) course is being taught at four levels at the same time. It is being taught in some viable Govt. schools, Intermediate colleges (private), degree colleges and even in Post-graduate colleges.

The teaching of degree standard (+3) (Pass and Hons.) is done in about 300 hundred constituent colleges and in most of the 147 affiliated colleges in our State. There are also about one hundred more colleges that have applied for affiliation to different universities of Bihar. Only three decades ago, there were only five Constituent Colleges, *i.e.* Patna College, Patna Science College, L.S. College, Muzaffarpur, Ranchi College, Ranchi and T.N.B. College, Bhagalpur in the whole of the State. Subsequently a few more colleges were raised to Constituent status (by a rough estimate 2-3 colleges per university). Most of these colleges had rich academic heritage with high traditions and efficient teachers. These colleges by virtue of their being Constituent were run and managed by the respective universities. The rest of the colleges were only affiliated to their respective universities. These colleges used to be managed by their respective governing bodies. In 1980, almost all the colleges were made Constituent by the government. Although in most of these colleges, the academic standard was poor and much below the mark. Many of these colleges do not have even proper accommodation for holding classes.

The Post-graduate teaching, till recently, was mainly confined to the University departments only but since 1985, the government has started Post-graduate teaching in a large number of colleges. The number of such colleges in presently three in Patna University, five in Bhagalpur University, six in Bihar University, five in L.N. Mithila University, seven in Magadh University and seven in Ranchi University , thus bringing the total number of P.G. Colleges at present to thirty-three. The most unfortunate matter in this regard is that the respective universities were not at all consulted before the government decided to start Post-graduate teaching in these colleges. These P.G. centres have been opened under a specific condition that the state government will not bear any financial liability regarding Post-graduate teaching at these centres. In essence, it means that the highest education in the State can be imparted without any financial investment by the State. In this sad state of affairs, one wonders as to what type of Post-graduates this State expects to produce without any financial input. One wonders also as to how the Government wants to bring quality in higher education by providing Post-graduate teaching in Commerce, Arts and Science subjects when many of these colleges do not have the infrastructure even for B.A. Pass and Honours teaching.

There is a provision in our State of an Inter University Board headed by a Chairman. Its main function is to draw the syllabuses of different subjects of all universities of the State to maintain uniformity in syllabuses and teaching schedule. But its role, in recent years, has not been up-to-mark . With the introduction of 10+2+3 system in our State, it was entrusted to draw the syllabuses for degree courses. The syllabuses drawn by this August body are not imaginative and for all practical purposes not every useful;. Moreover, the courses for degree classes of all subjects have been upgraded to Honours standard. General students have to study only for two years to get the B.A. degree and only those who secure a minimum of 45% marks and wish to offer Honours in the subject will have to study for the third year. So it is not 10+2+3 as envisaged in the new scheme, but 10+2+2+1.

If this indigenous concept of +3 (*i.e.* 2+1) is practised, it will take a student at least four years to clear a 3-year course, because every university in the State takes 8 to 10 months time to conduct pass course examinations, a student will have to wait for sometime before he is admitted to the Hons. Course. The proposed Honours Courses are so heavy that most of the colleges will not be able to complete them within 9-10 months time.

So far as the position of English in the new syllabus is concerned it has been reduced to the point of insignificance and oblivion in the sense that it has been given the status of an optional paper. A student can pursue his three years course without offering English. The syllabus of English drawn by this board for the pass course students is of Honours standard. It can feed the craving of a few students who want to specialise in English literature. Majority of students need to have some knowledge of English language as its knowledge is indispensable for higher studies in the field of science, commerce and even humanities. The study of English as a language has become all the more important in a developing country like ours. No body can deny its importance even as a linguafranca between the north and the south. The little knowledge which our students acquire upto Intermediate standard is by no logic sufficient. As the majority of college students come from the rural areas, where the standard of teaching English is very low, they have been making up their deficiency in English language at the degree stage up-till-now. they are expected to compete with their counterparts in Convent and public institutions at the time of seeking entrance in all India services and big business house after graduation. Definitely the students coming out form Convents and public schools are better than most of their counterparts from the countryside schools. But new syllabus has no provision for teaching of English as a language. In our view, English should be retained as a compulsory subject at degree level. At the same time, the syllabus of English should be made less formidable and attractive. The teaching of English at this stage does not mean teaching of English literature.

One of the reasons for the declining standard of teaching English in Bihar is the inability of teachers to understand the difference between the teaching of literature and the teaching of language skills. Everybody knows that the study of a language is not an end in itself, it is a means to develop one's power of expression and comprehension. This power of expression and comprehension can be achieved by mastering stylistic elements of the language. We agree with A.K. Sharma when he says:

> The main problem before a teacher of English in India, where we learn and teach English as a second language, is not 'how to teach' but 'what to teach' : that is , which of the two contents, namely, conceptual and stylistic, deserves more attention and emphasis? English language teaching in India, you will agree with me, has suffered a lot—so much so that our students who pass Intermediate and degree examinations with English either as a compulsory or as an elective subject, can neither speak nor write correct English. May be, because the emphasis

in our schools and colleges has always been on the conceptual content and the stylistic content has been neglected so far.[1]

Therefore, the syllabus for English should be made to develop students' power of expression and comprehension, but the newly drawn syllabus of English for degree classes is literature oriented. Moreover, English has been omitted altogether from the syllabus of B. Com. Can a student of Bihar compete with the students of other states in getting employment in business concerns or in preparing for chartered accountancy or cost accountancy without a good knowledge of English? The 'pass without English' policy of a previous government has already done great damage to the cause of education in our State and it will further drag the already backward Bihar to still more backwardness.

Although the universities in Bihar have accepted Hindi as medium of instruction, it should not be interpreted to mean that English should altogether be abolished from the universities. Owing to this narrow view, insufficient attention has been paid to the study of English in colleges under all the universities of Bihar. It would be unwise to discard English till Hindi is ready to play the role of common language that is now being played by English. Here we want to clarify that until and unless Hindi is accepted as the language of instruction by all educational institutions at all India basis, to discard English or to lessen its importance will not be in our interest. Let us try to understand the situation that will arise in the wake of our not knowing this language. In the absence of a common language (English occupies this place in India), the recruitment of the best men from any part of the country will not be possible. The students of Bihar will not be able to study in the university of their choice. The five Indian Institutes of Technology which can compete with any technical institution anywhere in the world hold a common entrance examination, have a common medium of instruction and recruit teachers

1. A.K. Sharma, "The Art of Writing Lesson in English for Correspondence Course", in B.K. Sinha (ed.) *Lesson Writing of Correspondence Students* (Institute of Correspondence Courses, Patna University, Patna, 1982), p. 95.

on an all India basis. If each candidate is permitted to use his own regional language as the medium of examination, the basis of competition and selection can be regional, not national. Our intention is never to see Hindi as a regional language. It is our national language and it should be developed to take the place of English, but it is for the people of other states to accept Hindi as their national language and give it its due place. The only thing that we want to emphasize is that both Hindi and English are essential. We cannot neglect English without harming the cause of education in our State. But we should also accept that English is not going to play the role, as it did before Independence. As it is an international language, we have to learn it as a second language. With the introduction of 10+2+3 system, we have seen that English has not been given due place in Bihar. V.V. Yardi feels that " with the introduction of the New Pattern of Education (ten years of instruction in school, two years in junior college, and three years in senior college), English in most states and union territories of India has virtually ceased to be a second language. It is expected that before long all the states and union territories of India may adopt this new pattern and, as a consequence, a uniform policy with regard to the teaching of English might emerge. When this comes about, English will have acquired the status of third language for all practical purposes although in the Hindi speaking areas it may nominally be designated L_2".[2] Yardi wants to suggest that we should reconsider our aims and objectives and method of teaching English in India because,

> A learner who is learning his L_2 is in a bilingual situation; if he is learning his L_3, he is in multilingual situation. In the acquisition of L_2 no serious problems are involved, comparatively speaking as interference stemming from one language...... can easily be contained. In the acquisition of L_3 the interference is likely to be doubled since the learner has already acquired two languages. The nature of interference, too, is of a different character in the case of L_3 learner. Given such a situation, the objectives of teaching

2. V.V. Yardi, " Teaching English as a third language: Some theoretical considerations" in *Forum XVI, 3,* (July, 1978), p. 38.

> English may have to shift from the acquisition of active skills to the acquisition of passive skills. And this may necessitate a departure from the methodology that traditionally includes the mastery of all four language skills.[3]

But at the same time scholars like Haugen, Weinreich and Vildomec[4] do not find much differences in approaches to the teaching of a second/third language. They do not suggest drastic changes on our aims and objectives and methodology of English language teaching in India.

Now let us decide what should be the objective of teaching English at the college stage. It is of paramount importance that the teacher should know what his task is and what he is trying to achieve by teaching English. In schools, we find some planning about what to teach and when to teach it mentioned specifically in the syllabus itself, but in the syllabuses of colleges, we do not have such directions. It is for the teacher to decide how and when to teach a particular teaching item. Thus, they want to cover the course without realising its aims and objectives. They believe to go on with their job of teaching without knowing the difficulties of the learner. The teacher should be fully aware of the fact that his students' proficiency in English it not upto mark owing to the deteriorating standard of teaching in schools. Our intermediate students are expected to have mastered at least 213 odd structures and about 2500 English vocabulary items when they pass their matriculation examination, but the reality is that they can hardly use 100 structures and 1000 vocabulary items. According to the report of the study conducted by Dr. D. Thakur and Dr. K.P. Thakur :

> "the students in Bihar at the beginning of the Pre-University Course had, on an average, the recognition knowledge of only 1393. words. They report that 60% of the students who took the vocabulary text had the recognition of only 942 words out of the total of 4619 words in our list...... only 10% of the students had the recognition knowledge of about 3000 words as suggested

---

3. *Ibid.*, pp. 38-9.
4. See, Veroboj Vildomec, *Multilingualism* (Leyden : A.W. Sythoff, 1963).

by Srinagar Conference of English teacher held in 1961".[5]

Our objectives of teaching English, therefore, should be practical and in keeping with the standard of proficiency achieved by our students. When the medium of instruction in our universities is no longer English , it is necessary to emphasize that the main aim of teaching English is to develop the ability of students to read and understand books, journals and reference materials in English. This does not mean that the skills of speaking and writing should be overlooked. What we want to emphasize is that only grand objective will not improve the standard of teaching in colleges. To quote Dr. Walker Hill :

> "Since any meaningful objective of education implies some change in the characteristics or competencies of students, it is to the students that we must look for evidence of its achievement. And in order to find such evidence, we must know that we are looking for. We must determine what characteristics we should expect to find in students in whom the objective is realized. Having thus formulated our goal in concrete terms, we can plan learning experiences which seem likely to lead to development of these characteristics. And we can devise means of assessing the extent to which they have been developed".[6]

The primary aim, therefore, of teaching of teaching English at this stage should be to concentrate on the fundamental skills of the language ability of the students, namely listening, speaking, reading and writing. At the end of Intermediate Course or even degree course, too, a student should be able to—

(i) understand a talk on a subject of general interest;

(ii) (a) carry on a natural conversation with clarity of expression on a topic within his experience;

(b) arrange, present, and explain his ideas intelligently on a topic selected by him:

---

5. Dr. D. Thakur and Dr. K.P. Thakur, " The Recognition of Vocabulary of P.U.C. Students in Bihar: A Reference Manual for textbook writers," Paper presented at the five-day seminar on Materials Production, CIEFL, Hyderabad, February, 1975.
6. Walker H. Hill, *Improvement of examinations* (Calicut: University of Calicut, 1972), p. 1.

(iii) understand the main statements or ideas in a written passage and be able to reproduce them, in the order in which they are given, in a simple workman like manner, and

(iv) express himself in writing with relevance and accuracy on

(a) a subject of general interest within his experience;

(b) a topic chosen from a subject within curriculum which entails a vocabulary relating specially to that branch of knowledge.

After discussing what should be the objectives of teaching English in college of Bihar, now let us examine whether the methods and techniques used by the teachers of English are faulty and out of date. The programme of teaching a second language can be implemented through the instrumentality of efficient methods and techniques. Of course, good teachers are more important than good methods, but an efficient teacher can improve remarkably the quality of teaching by applying good methods and techniques to teaching. Teachers of English in Bihar have been teaching through Grammar translation method and they have not departed from the beaten track up till now. In schools, too, we found during our survey that teachers were not taking interest in the structural approach of teaching English and surprisingly enough, they were translating the English structures which were meant for practice and drill by the students. In colleges, too, the teacher comes to the class and takes one of the textbooks prescribed in the syllabus, opens it and starts reading himself and then tells the meaning of some lines in Hindi. The students who have been taught English through Hindi in their schools find no distinction between the teachers of English in school and colleges. One thing which he finds at the Intermediate level is that he forgets the structures which he had learnt in the school, because he does not have to learn new structures at this stage.

There are also some teachers who teach English through the medium of English itself and think that any word of Hindi spoken in the class-room will be against the convention of teaching English. Thus, they teach through direct method. All these practices are due to the fact that they do not have clear cut objectives before them. They believe in lecturing whether it benefits the students or not. They are conservative in their approach and they are not ready to learn any new methods and techniques of teaching English.

It is essential , therefore for every college teacher to obtain a copy of English syllabus for schools. He will find in it a list of all structures that his students are supposed to have learnt in schools. If he can discipline himself to use only these structures when talking to his class and ask questions that can be answered in these structures, he will both help his students to improve their mastery of them and also help himself to discover those which are least well handled by his students. While correcting the students' faulty sentences, he may well find it useful to refer to the basic pattern which the student is trying to use. He will also find it useful to pick out certain patterns from the passages the students have to study in their college course and make sure that they know how to use them. Thus, we see that if a college teacher is familiar with the school syllabus he will be in a position to help his students to improve their English. One of the tasks of the college teacher is remedial work on these structures. But we do not find that college teachers take interest in this regard.

The next important problem of teaching English in colleges is bad textbooks. There is a mistaken idea that the standard of English is raised by the prescription of difficult books. Speed in reading can be achieved only through the provision of books which students can read with comprehension. Where books are beyond the ready comprehension of students, a distaste for reading is created. This unfortunate attitude is one of the obstacles which the college teacher has to overcome. This is also one of the reasons why a sort of reform in the syllabus is badly needed.

The methods of teaching English in both the schools and colleges of Bihar vary from teacher to teacher and from institution to institution, and this is also one of the reasons for the deterioration in the students' acquisition of proficiency in English. If we listen to a lesson conducted through translation method we discover that more than half the time is spent in using the mother-tongue and the total time spent in the use of English, including both listening and speaking, is only 25 minutes out of a period of 45 minutes. There may appear to be a better understanding of the passage being studied this way, but the students, in fact, learn less English than they would have done if the teacher had taught the passage by techniques which use questions, illustrations and simple practice drills.

University syllabuses[7] do not fully satisfy the present objectives of the teaching of English. Books are often prescribed which reflect English life and culture and are less understood and appreciated by students. Books containing common vocabulary and common themes would have been more useful. A prose book about physical and social sciences may be more useful. The purpose of any prose book is to enable the students to develop the stock of words and thus such words as can be used in day-to-day life are certainly more useful. The introduction of the plays of Shakespeare at degree level (simple pass course) is not practical. Because to teach Shakespeare to the students who are not sound in linguistic skills is nothing but to try to make a super-structure on sandy foundations. Although literature teaching is one of the ways of language teaching but to teach difficult books to the students of B.A. (pass) course is not practicable. To quote Halliday, McIntosh and Strevens:

> Whatever may have been the effect in British schools and universities of denying or playing down the importance of language and linguistics in English studies, the effect abroad has been to encourage a process of self-annihilation in which more and more literature has been accompanied by less and less language ability until in many overseas countries the study of ' English' in the sense of 'English literature' has become a practical impossibility in the present educational circumstances.[8]

If it is prescribed in any case, it should be taught in such a manner that students may understand it well. Students are generally greatly handicapped in the power of self expression, therefore, great emphasis should be given on language courses which may consist of essay writing, letter writing, precise

7. See. Appendix II.
8. M.A.K. Halliday, Angus MacIntosh and Peter Strevens, *op. cit.*, p. 184.

writing, grammar and syntax. At degree courses, literary pieces should be selected from modern literature. Students should also be taught contemporary usages. While teaching correct pronunciation and phonetic transcription, teachers should be cautious about the stress and intonation of his own speech. English courses should also be extended to B.Com. and B.Sc. students.

The greatest casualty in the teaching of English at the college level is the teaching of grammar. During our survey we found that in majority of colleges teachers teaching English to the Intermediate Classes cared to cover four books prescribed in English Paper I and cared little of Paper II, which is the most important part of the syllabus at the Intermediate stage. The students in some colleges also voiced their concern over this and said that teachers knowingly did not teach grammar for their private tuitions. The reasons were if students were not taught grammar at colleges, they would have no option but to contact such teachers who believed in and practised private tuition at their residences. It is really a shameful commentary on the part of the teachers of English. We suggest in this connection that private tuition by college teachers should be completely banned. On the other hand, teachers usually say that they have to cover the text-books prescribed in the syllabus and, thus, they find no time for grammar teaching. But it is also a fact that teachers want to something in the class and so far as grammar teaching is concerned, they think it a tedious job, without realising the fact that without attaining linguistic skill, students cannot appreciate literature. It is obvious that this situation cannot be met by the traditional teaching method of lecturing, although the college teachers of English do not find it convenient to shift to any other teaching method.

The question to be dealt with at this stage is why the teaching of linguistic skills is considered difficult at the college level. We found during our survey that the size of the classes everywhere was considerably large (not less than 150 students) and, thus, students' participation in the class work was quite impossible. The ratio of students in relation to teachers was not proportionate. This is one of the reasons why individual attention is not paid to students. For individual attention, there is provision of tutorial classes but the number of students in tutorial classes also is again very large, because most of the colleges can afford neither so many rooms for this purpose, nor so many teachers to conduct efficient teaching of English. Thus, until it is recognized that language teaching needs provision, similar to, if not more than, that for science subjects, large scale improvement is not possible. It is a recognised fact that English is a skill subject and it needs practical work. In various science subjects, practical work demands a definite limit to the size of the class. It should also be recognised that the practical work in the teaching of English demands that the number of students in the class be limited.

This is the crux of the difference between the study of language and literature. Within reasonable limits, a lecture on literature in general or on a specific book can be given to a class of any size. The students' main activity is listening. But the teaching of language cannot be conducted through lecture method alone. Listening is not adequate as a student's activity. There must be an active use of language, for which students' participation is necessary.

The teaching of English in colleges is understood to be the teaching of English literature only and the points of linguistic interest are generally ignored. It is a fact that most of the college teachers have failed to improve the standard of teaching English at this stage because of their literary bias. They fail to understand that those who are not linguistically equipped are unable to understand lectures in English. Though some of the college teachers have received training at CIEFL, Hyderabad, and attended Summer Institutes and Refresher Courses organised by U.G.C., they do not get encouragement or opportunity to practice the techniques. It is also a fact that out college teachers think themselves above training and they do not want to be trained in the recent methods of teaching. We may quote a passage from the *Report of English Review Committee* to make our point more clear :

> Several universities have recommended that there should be a course in a linguistics at B.A. and M.A. stage what is necessary is not linguistics or applied linguistics as much as a course in modern English usage, its vocabulary, morphology, syntax and phonetics. It is only when such a

> course is introduced in our B.A. or M.A. syllabus in English that we should produce teachers who will be able to teach the English language in our schools and colleges. In fact it would be most economical to break the vicious circle at this end, since training thousand of school teachers will take a long time and may not be fully achieved. Our M.A.'s in English are at present able to teach the poetry of Keats. But they are unable to teach the ABC of English usage. ......It is desirable that all teachers of English should receive some training at the Central Institute of English, Hyderabad and when this is not possible to attend special summer course organised by the University.[9]

In view of the facts stated above, college teachers of English should throw off the sense of apathy, if any, from their mind against being trained in language teaching. The role of linguistics in the teaching of English in India and elsewhere has been widely debated but it has been found that linguistics can help a lot in the teaching of a language. Today, we have to read more and more subjects to solve the problems facing our education system. What A.H. Marckwardt says is very appropriate and meaningful and we fully agree with him :

> Over the past two decades, education in this country and indeed elsewhere has felt the impact of two explosions: an explosion of population and an explosion of knowledge. The first has resulted in the number of children to be taught often without corresponding facilities. The second has made it necessary to teach more subjects and more about the familiar subjects also without a corresponding increase in the time necessary to perform this extended task. In each of the various discipline—mathematics, science, social studies, foreign language, knowledge has expanded rapidly. In addition, new approaches and new methods of teaching these subjects have been developed.[10]

We have to keep pace with the ever increasing areas of knowledge. To quote Marckwardt again:

---

9. *Report of the English Review Committee* (University Grants Commission, New Delhi, 1965), p. 35.
10. Albert H. Marckwardt : *Linguistics the Teaching of English*, Indian University Press, Bloomington (London, 1966), p. 3.

> In case of English, the teachers of this subject like their colleagues in other departments are faced with a multitude of recent developments in the systematic study language. This body of knowledge and systematic procedure of study is what we have come to know as linguistics. It is not a fact that linguistics will furnish quick and easy answers to problems which have been plaguing English teachers for years, but there can be no question about the value for every teacher of becoming acquainted with various ways of looking at language in a new perspective.[11]

The teachers of English must know linguistics, because they have to fact the every changing curricula. The approaches to teaching English have kept on changing from the very beginning, teaching English as a second language does not at all mean teaching English literature only. We shall have to revise our aims and objectives and try to lay more emphasis on developing linguistic skills of the students. A.K. Sharma also thinks so when he says:

> The linguistic analysis and mastery of a poem or prose piece is more valuable for an Intermediate or degree student than any aesthetic consideration or biographical and psychological speculation about the author. An awareness of the different groups to which words belong and the relative significance of these groups of words from the viewpoint of second language learning, a clear idea or phonemes, enorphemes, word phrases, clauses and sentences, a close and detailed comprehension of idiomatic and figurative styles, and of dialects and registers—all these are far more relevant at this sage than any abstract or philosophical speculation, an exercise in pedantry for which Intermediate or degree students have not been trained. Emphasis on language oriented teaching of English at these levels is bound to produce better result.[12]

Linguistics helps us in selecting the methods of teaching, in judging the usefulness of a particular method. "A method of teaching a subject will depend on what the teacher

---

11. *Ibid.*
12. A.K. Sharma, "The Art of Writing Lessons in English for Correspondent Students", *op. cit.*, p. 95.

believes the nature of that subject to be; similarly a method of teaching language will depend on what you believe in the nature of language. If you believe the teaching language is teaching a skill, then you try to organise your teaching to fit that idea".[13]

Intermediate students, in this way, should be taught in such a way that they may learn the mechanics of expression consisting of sentence pattern, spelling and punctuation. The students should be encouraged to write essays consisting of about 250 words or paragraphs of 100 words or develop stories from given outlines. Due place should be given to tutorial work but it is really sad to not that tutorial classes in most of the colleges in Bihar, are done on papers only. There must have been two tutorial classes a week. One tutorial should provide for written exercise to improve written composition and the other should aim at improving the proficiency of students in spoken English. Teachers who take up the spoken English tutorial classes will have to be carefully selected for their own fitness to take up the work. If the syllabus for Intermediate classes is taught properly, we are sure to achieve our aims and objectives. Textbooks prescribed should be divided into feasible home assignments and during the tutorial periods, the answers of home assignments may be discussed. Gokak also lays emphasis on the linguistics attainments of students:

> The text should be primarily studied from the language point of view, promoting the expansion of general and specific vocabulary, comprehension and correct expression.[14]

We have five lecture periods a week for the teaching of English in colleges, but in most of the colleges, classes are not held owing to the lack of adequate number of teaching staff. In majority of colleges classes are frequently suspended on flimsy grounds and, sometimes even for want to space.

Owing to the absence of an atmosphere conducive to the growth of higher education in most of the colleges, the standard of teaching has deteriorated. Nobody is interested

13. June Derrick : *Teaching English to Immigrants* (Organiser, Schools Council Project in English for Immigrant children), (Longman, 1966), p. 66.
14. V.K. Gokak, *op. cit.*, p. 104.

in ensuring maximum teaching hours in colleges and universities departments. Even the Government is more concerned about examinations and attached little significance to teaching. So far as examinations are concerned all the examinations at Hons. and Post-graduate levels are conducted by external examiners. The answer-sceipts are sent to examiners after confidential coding. So far as the examinations of Intermediate and degree classes are concerned, they are held only at those colleges which are selected as centres of examination; still mass scale use of unfair means is reported from the majority of the college of the State. Classes a suspended during the period of these examinations and then comes the evaluation of answerscripts of Intermediate and graduation examinations. Here also, there are some teachers in almost all the universities of Bihar, who have been contributing to the erosion of right kind of values from our academic life. Many of them are corrupt in their conduct and behaviour. It has been seen that such teachers who are engaged in private tuition or associated with coaching institutes on commercial lines encourage the penetration of corrupt and dishonest practices into the academic life on the campus. It is mostly these teachers who reduce centralised evaluation of answerbooks to a state of farce. They can never be serious examiners. A lot of their time is spent in making *pairwi* and they evaluate their part of answerbooks without caring for the merit and demerit of the answerscripts. If a particular answer is of 10 marks, they would award 6½ and if it is of 7 they would award 3½ (*i.e.* not often in round figures) to give credibility to their marking. But the reality is that they finish their work very soon to do what they consider their primary duty (*i.e.* Pairwi). Such examiners should be debarred permanently from examination and evaluation work.

As the problem of teaching English is linked with the problems of education in general, we cannot overlook the harsh realities of our State. When we are dealing with the problems of teaching English in the Colleges of Bihar, we must know what type of college to college. Not only in colleges of Patna University but in some premier colleges of other universities of our State, the teaching standard has not deteriorated to the extent it has in most of the colleges located in rural areas and newly converted constituent colleges. During our visit to one of such colleges a student told us that the writer of the poem, entitled "Where the Mind is without Fear" was Rabindra Nath Tagore and he belonged to England because he had composed English poems. This was his knowledge of English literature and when he was asked to explain the word 'they', his answer was surprising that 'they' was third person, singular number. This type of answer can be found even from the answerbooks of Intermediate examinations. These days answerbooks of the students of Intermediate classes are not examined on the basis of what they have written (if the examination is fair), but on the basis of what they want to write. It is the duty of the examiner to guess what the examinee wants to communicate. Therefore, we should try hard to teach English language, and not waste our time discussing English literature.

In Bihar, as we have already seen, English is not a compulsory subject in the three-year degree course. It is, however, a fact that more than 75% students offer this English as one of the subjects of their combination. There are three papers of 100 marks each. The syllabus[15] of English of almost all universities is on the same pattern.

Paper I	Poetry and Drama
Paper II	Miscellaneous Prose
Paper III	Grammar and Composition

When we examine the books prescribed for teaching English to degree students, we find them literature oriented, seeing the standard of the achievement of Intermediate students, the syllabus designed for degree students is somewhat difficult for average students. Obvious as it is, majority of students will not become teachers of English in schools, colleges and universities. They would rather join other professions where knowledge of English literature is not needed. They acquire more drilling in writing precis or reporting speeches made at different places of public importance. Therefore some of the books of literature should be replaced by such books as are relevant from the viewpoint of composition and usage. All students will not benefit simply

15. See, Appendix II.

by acquainting themselves with the various genres of English literature and their respective merits and excellences. Writing literary appreciation of poems will not be of much utility to general students.

In the Chapter 'Why study literature?' in his book *Thinking about English,* Michael Paffard quotes an eloquent passages from the Report of Board of Education in 1921 on the teaching of English in England :

> English literature is the 'sublimation of human thought, passion, feeling', that it 'is concerned with issues which are of universal interest', that it 'introduces the student to great minds and new forms of experience' and is a means of contact with great minds, the channel by which to draw upon their experience with profit and delight'.[16]

Perhaps, influenced by the above mentioned passage, our course framers have put enough of English literature in degree (pass course) classes. Students at this stage need enough of introductory lectures, so that they may understand the fundamentals of English literature. First of all the students, with so many books to go through at this stage, must know the essentials of literature and then the history of English literature. Until and unless they know the social history of England, they cannot understand and appreciate the poems prescribed in their syllabus. In almost all the colleges of all the universities of Bihar, students have to read at least 28 poems by 28 different poets ranging from William Shakespeare (Elizabethan period) to W.B. Yeats and T.S. Eliot (Modern Age). They are also expected to read one tragedy of Shakespeare and a comedy of G.B. Shaw or some other modern dramatists. In the second paper, they have to go through an English novel and two anthologies, one each of essays and stories. In Paper I, they have also to study a mock-epic poem. Thus, a Bachelor of Arts (Pass) students is expected critically to appreciate poems and evaluate the tragic significance of the tragedies of William Shakespeare. For this reason or that, such a vast course of English language and literature becomes unmanageable in most of the colleges of

16. Michael Paffard : *Thinking About English* (London : Ward Lock Educational, 1978), p. 70.

Bihar. And this we think is one of the reasons why students take recourse to cheap notes and use unfair means in the examinations. Prescribing standard books in the syllabus, thus, is no solution to the problem, rather it adds to the problem in many ways. What is required is that the course objectives and linguistic objectives must first be made clear and books be prescribed accordingly. Unless this is done, we should not expect our teaching to yield much result. Literature of the sake of literature should not be put in the syllabus. Literature can be enjoyed only by those who have mastered the linguistic skills of the language. Michael Paffard puts it :

> Teaching literature, it is felt, must be centrally concerned with notions like appreciation, enjoyment, response, insight, interpretation, critical discrimination and judgment. It is much less clear whether and how these less exclusively and straightforwardly cognitive capacities can or should be taught, or tested. Indeed, it is often said that 'appreciation—the key term—is caught rather than taught.[17]

If the course is not simplified, it would be a problem for the students of B.A. (Pass course) to pursue their study of English, and consequently most of the students would offer another subject in its place. It is advisable, therefore, that a language oriented syllabus of English be introduced for the students of degree classes. Literature oriented syllabus should be prescribed for the Honours and Post-graduate students. Majority of the students offer English at graduation level with a view to improving their knowledge of the language. They do not simply have the capacity to enjoy and appreciate the beauty and richness of English literature. There is, therefore, no harm in being realistic and call a spade a spade. It would have been appreciated by all and sundry if a paper of General English consisting of 100 marks is introduced for the B.A., B.Com. and B.Sc. students. This, we are sure, would have gone a long way in bringing improvement in the students' knowledge of the English language. The teaching of English at Honours and Post-graduate level is confined mostly to

17. Michael Paffard, *op. cit.*, pp.76-77.

the premier educational institutions of Bihar. There used to be six papers of English for Honours teaching in colleges of Bihar but with the introduction of the 10+2+3 system which in practice is 10+2+2+1; the teaching of Honours is yet to start. There shall be five papers to be taught within a period of one year at the Honours stage. We are afraid whether these five papers would be covered within a year. The educational institutions in Bihar are practically closed for half the year on account of various holidays and vacations.

Generally English Honours classes present a chaotic jumble of good and bad students. Some of them are really good but a large number of them are quite hopeless. The students of English Honours are expected to know the essentials of literature as well as the socio-political history of England. A teacher has no option but to pity the lot of these students who have neither the sense of language nor the sense of imagination. To boost, they do not even get books in the market. College Libraries also present a decent book. Thus, the teaching of English Honours in most of the colleges of Bihar is done without books and journals. The main source from where the Honours students acquire their knowledge of English literature is the age-old notes prepared by teachers with a view to earning money by selling them to their head-strong students. The greatest fraud among the teachers of English attracts the largest crowd of students under his tabulate. Those students who cannot afford to be under the private tutelage of 'teachers mostly depend on cheap bazaar notes. The intelligent ones, however, whether they gather material from teachers or from the cheap bazaar notes, try to improve their answers by adding points and quoting passages from whatever standard critical material is available to them. The dull ones, on the other hand, do nothing of this sort, rather they make certain grammatical and spelling mistakes in both copying these notes and reproducing them in the examinations. They do not ever try to understand English language and literature of their own. One of the factors responsible for this deterioration is the pattern of question-setting. It is easy to predict. What questions would be asked on what books in which examination. The students simply have to memorize. The teacher also teaches only those aspects which are important for the examinations. Students, thus, are not given proper orientation, and teachers are to blame for this. They do for their students what the students themselves are supposed to do. What Bruce Pattison suggests in this connection is worth quoting :

> We should never do anything our pupils can do for themselves, some works can entirely be left to them. We may find it necessary to check whether the works have been read, or if any part of them has remained obscure but that is testing not teaching.[18]

Students of English Honours are expected to be proficient in spoken English as well. They should also possess the ability to develop the power of written and oral expression in a classroom situation. This will help all students in general and those in particular who, after passing graduation with English Honours, want to join teaching profession in schools. The students of English Honours should also attain distinction in debates and symposia. For their participation in these activities, they should be awarded extra marks. It is possible only if some marks are reserved for internal tests.

The post-graduate teaching of English in Bihar now is not confined only to the university departments. It has been for some years started in different degree college, where no extra hand, fund, building and library facilities have been provided. The main problem before the teachers of these colleges is that they are over-burdened. They have to teach right from the Intermediate courses to the Post-graduate courses, which is not possible without sufficient number of hands. When teachers go on leave, the teaching in the periods assigned to them is automatically suspended, and this hampers teaching irreparably. Classes are also suspended when these colleges hold university examinations for Intermediate and Bachelor students, for in majority of these colleges there are no separate examination halls. Post- teaching, it may be pointed out here, in the colleges of Bihar, is opened on political considerations

---

18. Bruce Pattison : "Some Notes on the Teachering of Literature", in *E.L.T. Selection I* (ed.) W:R. Lee (London : Oxford University Press, 1967), p. 175.

rather than on academic considerations. The Government of Bihar has made a joke of Post-graduate teaching.

By and large ten syllabuses of teaching English at the P.G. level in different Universities of Bihar are framed on the same pattern. The distribution of papers is something like :

Paper I	— The Renaissance including Drama
Paper II	— The Eighteenth Century
Paper III	— The Nineteenth Century
Paper IV	— Applied Criticism
Paper V	— Modern literature
Paper VI	— Middle English literature
Paper VII	— An essay (literary)
Paper VIII	— Special Paper—A prescribed author or Drama or American literature or Linguistics

A Study group appointed by the Ministry of Education has suggested that special papers may be offered from among the following :

(A)

1. History of English language.
2. Problems involved in the teaching of English as a second language.
3. More advanced topics in the phonetics of English and in structural linguistics, with special reference to English.

The above mentioned courses may be taken up by Higher Secondary teachers of English or by lecturers in compulsory English.

(B)

This may be taken up particularly by lecturers in English literature.

Any three of the following course units :

1. Indo-Anglian literature.
2. American literature.
3. Old English literature.

4. Middle English literature.
5. English literature in the 15th century.[19]

Thus we see that we need so many courses to be included in our M.A. (English) syllabuses to make the teaching and learning at this stage more useful, meaningful and up-to-date. Gokak suggests in this regard that it would be more beneficial if we include courses like the theory of education and the theory of curriculum construction, etc. As he puts it :

> It would be ideal if those who decide to become college teachers in any subject are given a six month course in the theory of education and in curriculum construction and test procedures, after they take their M.A. degree. A good part of the antiquated nature of our syllabuses, the mechanical nature of our teaching and the rigidity of our examinational procedures are due to the fact that our collegiate teachers lack such training and become examiners and members of boards of studies and other academic bodies without being equipped for their task.[20]

To achieve the aims and objectives set for Post-graduate students we shall have to equip our P.G. Colleges and University departments with sufficient and qualified teachers, buildings, libraries and language laboratories. For all this, adequate financial assistance from the State Government and the U.G.C. is needed.

---

19. The study of English in India, *op. cit.*, p. 33.
20. V.K. Gokak, *op. cit.*, p. 123.

5 The Problems of Teaching English in Training Colleges

Teacher Education and Training are of great importance. Over the years, he dearth of trained teachers in the field of English as a second language teaching has been greatly felt. As teaching is an art, the skills of teaching can be acquired by dint of practice in doing teaching. But in most of the training colleges of Bihar, practice teaching is not found adequate to equip student-teachers with new methods of teaching English as a second language. The syllabus of teacher-education in general is not up-to-date. It lays more emphasis on theoretical studies. R.C. Srivastav and K. Bose rightly maintain :

> It appears that the teacher education centres in India, by and large, prefer a routinised academic programme than a permissive exploratory one. Tutorials, assignments, tests and internal assessment are means to sharpen the skill of teaching. No wonder, the training colleges smack of traditionalism; experimentation that should be the hallmark of change is not much encouraged. A direction to the new education that should flow from such teacher training institutions is missing, the very purpose of the existence of such centres is being rightly questioned except that the justification is sought in the perpetuation of the old order.[1]

There are two streams of formal teacher education in Bihar. One is for training teachers to be employed in Elementary (Primary & Middle) schools and the other for training teachers for Secondary schools. In the first course, which is of two years duration leading to a certificate in teacher education, Secondary school certificate holders of those holding equivalent

1. R.C. Srivastav and K. Bose, *Theory and Practice of Teacher Education in India* (Allahabad, Chugh Publications, 1978), p. 44.

qualifications are trained in eighty-four training institutes[2] set up and maintained by the State Government. These institutes are now called Primary Teachers' Education Colleges. These are at least twelve other training institutes set up and maintained by non-government agencies.

In the second course, which is of ten months duration, graduates are trained for teaching in Secondary schools. This course leads to Bachelor's degree in Education. The course is conducted in two colleges (Patna Training College and Women's Training College) under Patna University, Patna. There are about ten other colleges managed and maintained by the State Government and affiliated to different Universities of Bihar. Government Teacher Training College, Turki, and G.T.T. college. Chapra are affiliated to Bihar University, Muzaffarpur. Two colleges—one at Samastipur and the other at Saharsa are affiliated to L.N. Mithila University, Darbhanga. Government Teachers Training Colleges at Bhagalpur and Deoghar are affiliated to Bhagalpur University, Bhagalpur. Government Teachers Training Colleges at Ranchi and Hazaribagh and Women's Teachers Training College, Ranchi are affiliated to Ranchi University, Ranchi, and Government Teachers Training College, Gaya is affiliated to Magadh University, Bodh Gaya. There are also a few colleges maintained by non-government agencies. These are sub-standard institutions where practically no facilities worth the name are available for conducting the programme.

Let us, first of all, examine the aims and objectives of teaching English in these training colleges of Bihar . In Primary Teacher' Education Colleges, trainees have to study a few general subjects related to Educational Theory, Educational Management, etc. They have also to study Health and Hygiene, Mathematics and other language papers (mother-tongue, National language). English is not an important subject at this stage. It is not compulsory, rather it is an extra optional paper. Trainees, generally, do not opt for a course in English in these Colleges. What is advisable is that English ought to be made a popular, optional, if not compulsory, subject at this stage, for it is the products of these

2. *Annual Report 1984* (The State Council of Educational Research and Training , Patna), p. 54.

institutions who are entrusted with the job of teaching English to the beginners in Primary and Middle schools. One of the prime reasons of weak foundation of English teaching at Primary and Middle schools level, therefore, is the lack of proper training to teachers.

The aims and objectives of teaching English are clearly laid down in the syllabus meant for Primary Teachers' Education Colleges. These objectives are certainly lofty. To quote them will not be out of place here:

(1) To develop in the student-teacher the ability of *(a)* Listening *(b)* Speaking *(c)* Reading and Writing—all with understanding.

(2) To enable the student-teacher to understand that language learning is a matter of forming automatic language habits.

(3) To provide basic knowledge of and to give practice in the use of structures contained in the syllabus for classes V and VI (New).

(4) To enable the student-teacher to express themselves on matters of general interest within the range of their experience.

(5) To enable the student-teachers to understand books meant for general reading to prepare notes from reference books on methodology and pedagogy written in English.

(6) To provide the students a means for inter-state communication in India for the promotion of socio-cultural exchange resulting in emotional and national integration.[3]

What is required to achieve the aforesaid aims and objectives of teaching English at this stages, is that the teaching of English methodology in these colleges should at least be made a popular subject and taht efficient and qualified teachers should be posted to teach English to these student-teachers. The teaching of English methodology at this state is not given proper attention and that is why these student-teachers,

3. *Syllabus : Primary Teacher Education Colleges* (Education Department Government of Bihar, 1977), p. 76.

generally, do not offer English methodology. During our survey, we found that only one of the teachers of English was an M.A. in English. So, we can say that there is dearth of competent teachers to teach English in these colleges. In these training colleges, trained graduate teachers with some experience are appointed lectures, whereas teachers with Post-graduate qualification should have been appointed. Gokak also hints at this problem when he says:

> The staffing of training schools presents a most unsatisfactory state of affairs. It is apparently based on the notion that if graduates should be trained in training colleges, undergraduates should be trained in training schools. If trained M.A.'s are lectures in training college, trained graduates can be lectures in training schools.[4]

Teaching students of lower classes need better understanding and better knowledge. *The Report of the Secondary Education Commission (1972)* also lays emphasis on this aspect:

> It is an accepted principle that teaching in the lower standard requires as much, if not more, preparation as in the High Schools and that lower the grade of pupils the greater is the skill required to teach them..... the point to be emphasized is that proper education at this stage is not possible with the type of teachers as are now accepted for Primary Schools. If good foundation is to be laid at this most impressionable stage, efforts should be made to see that better equipped and better trained teachers are available.[5]

The present position of Primary Teachers' Education Colleges is alarming. The products of secondary schools are admitted into these colleges to be trained as future teachers for Primary as well as Middle Schools of Bihar. The standard of proficiency achieved by students passing matriculation examination, today, is not upto mark. They pose a big question mark before our Teacher Education Programme. They are so deficient in knowledge that they cannot even express themselves correctly in their mother-tongues. Therefore, the

4. V.K. Gokak, *op. cit.*, p. 92.
5. *Report of the Secondary Education Commission* (Government of India, 1972), p. 1961.

basic qualification for admission in these colleges should be +2 (Intermediate) or graduation and not matriculation. No doubt, the number of teachers is increasing day-by-day, but at the same time, efficiency in teaching and learning is decreasing at a rapid rate. Necessarily, there is something wrong with the Teacher Education Programme in our State.

Generally, the teacher-students at these colleges do not take much interest in their training programmes. There are so many reasons for this sad state of affairs. It is a fact that even after receiving training at these colleges, they have to wait for years together to get a job in a school and in this long wait, they forget everything which they learn during their training period. While they are at their training institutes, they are not provided with the facilities which a student-teacher is expected to enjoy for pursuing his studies smoothly.

The majority of the P.T.E. college libraries are ill-stocked and housed in inadequate or unattractive rooms. The teachers or clerks incharge of the library are not given library allowance and, thus they do not pay full attention to their work. It has also been noticed that the habits of study of teachers and trainees are not what they should be. As the teachers themselves are not interested in the use of library, students also remain in dark regarding library books. There is also no provision of reading rooms in most of the colleges. For creating a proper teaching and learning situation, it is essential that these colleges are provided with library facilities with permanent librarians and reading rooms. Teachers and students of these colleges should be encouraged to use the library for giving proper academic orientation to these institutions.

The syllabus[6] of English methodology of Primary Teachers' Training College is not up-to-date and it needs revision. Courses devised for them should be intended partly to improve their use of English and partly to equip them as teachers of English. By the time students come to training colleges, they have already had six to eight years' acquaintance with English. This is the time to go systematically over the language experiences they have already had. They should be

6. See, Appendix II.

in a better position to acquire an elementary knowledge of the structures of present day English. They should learn to use some intermediate as well as advanced structures. They are also expected to learn spoken English which should be free from mistakes.

During training period, trainees are expected to learn how to write correctly. Training in written expression should consist of exercises within the specified vocabulary and structures. They include—description of simple pictures, production of simple operations, implication of passages written in free English, writing letters and applications in simple English. For achieving these objectives, students should be encouraged to read a number of books in simple English. Efforts have been made to make the teaching of English more scientific and systematic through various research projects conducted at CIEFL, Hyderabad and other University centres and Training Colleges. Supplementary readers, a series of exercise books in English, handbooks for teachers and a set of wall pictures, flash cards and Gramophone records for the first three years of courses have been produced. The teachers at P.T.E. Colleges of Bihar should know about these developments and thereby tell their student-teachers to go through them. The most important thing regarding teaching is that the student-teachers must know what he is upto and how he is going to achieve it. The English syllabus must have scope for practice-teaching. In planning an English language teaching course, the following areas must be included :

(a) Development of the trainees' English proficiency.
(b) Relevant psycholinguistic and sociolinguistic study.
(c) Theoretical and/or descriptive linguistic study of language *per se*.
(d) Descriptive linguistic study of the English language—phonological, grammatical etc.
(e) Curriculum, materials and methods study, including the extent to which this should be ESP biased.
(f) Practical teaching, including observation of and participation in real and simulated teaching.[7]

7. Peter Wingard, "Training English lecturers in an overseas University," in R.R. Jordon (ed.), *Case Studies in ELT* (London. Collins ELT, 1983), p. 244.

The practice-teaching in English in these P.T.E. Colleges is of little importance. They are not taught a definite approach to the teaching of English. They do not get opportunity to become familiar with psychological principles of language learning and gain proficiency in using the various presentation and establishment techniques. These can be learnt through their day-to-day teaching.

The teachers of English of these colleges do not keep themselves abreast with the recent developments in the field of linguistics and theories of learning and teaching, without which they cannot teach their student-teachers about the usefulness of teaching aids and their application to the day-to-day teaching. the student-teachers must know the general principles of language teaching, the use of teaching aids, the methods and techniques of teaching and testing. The teaching of each item in the vocabulary, structures, exercise materials should be demonstrated practically.

The problem of the dearth of competent teachers can be solved to some extent if one lecturer, who has specialised in the method of teaching English, is appointed in each training college. It will help in imparting sound education to the student-teachers.

The time-allocation factor is also important. At present, there are only six English classes a week. They should, however, be twelve a week, and that will ensure better result. Regarding time-allocation for the content and the method course, the Report of the study group[8] appointed by the Ministry of Education says, "The Courses should be taught for a year with ten periods per week."

	Content	*Methods*
1st term (14 weeks)		
8 periods per week-Content	112	—
2 periods per week-Methods	—	28
2nd term (14 weeks)		
2 periods per week-Content	28	—
8 periods per week-Methods	—	112
Total	140	140
		280

8. The study of English in India (Ministry of Education, Government of India, 1967), p. 231.

While dealing with problem of teaching English in P.T.E. Colleges of Bihar, we have tried to suggest ways and means to improve the present situations. For fulfilling the aims and objectives of teaching English, appropriate steps must be taken in proportion to the prescribed curriculum and the needs of schools. The teachers coming out of these colleges are entrusted with the work of teaching children. Everybody knows that most of our middle schools of our State, even 'Madhyama' pass teachers are there to teach English. It is these teachers who lay foundations and teach the child the alphabet of the English language. This deficiency affects the quality of education in general and more particularly the teaching of a second language like English, which is spoken in the first language by very few people in the country.

For proper teaching in schools, proper training of teacher is essential. The student-teacher should be given all facilities so that they may become good teachers. They should be taught how to make a writing pattern and how to write in a good hand. Only then can they help their pupils to write a legible and beautiful hand; trainees should also acquire the ability to organize group work, because this saves time spent on the correction of scripts. They should also know how to acquire better pronunciation. For acquiring this ability, they must know the influence of the mother-tongue and other factors responsible for the deterioration in the teaching and learning of English pronunciation. Trainees should be given practice in pronunciation drills.

The student-teacher should acquire the ability "to use the following devices for presenting materials, situational teaching, the use of pictures, blackboard, drawing, wall-charts, dramatisation, language, games, songs and judicious use mother-tongue".[9]

II

The second type of teacher education in Bihar is meant for preparing teachers for secondary schools. We have tried to point out some of the burning problems of teaching English in Primary Teachers Education Colleges of Bihar and now we shall examine what ails our graduate teacher training centres.

9. The Study of English in India, (1967), p. 231.

The existing graduate/post-graduate teacher education institutions are of various type : *(i)* University departments or University Colleges of Education, *(ii)* Training Colleges directly controlled by the Education Department, Govt. of Bihar and affiliated to different universities, *(iii)* Private or Minority Colleges affiliated to different universities of the State. All these three types of educational institutions give courses leading to the degree of B.Ed.

We have, at present, two colleges under Patna University and ten colleges managed and maintained directly by the Government. There are also a few private or minority colleges managed by non-government agencies. About 1800 hundred graduates and post-graduates are admitted to these colleges every year, out of which nearly 1500 get Bachelor's degree in Education.

The graduate training (B.Ed.) course is of ten months duration. During this short period of training, the student-teacher is trained in methods of teaching covering at least two subjects. The student-teacher acquires theoretical knowledge of the method of teaching these subjects. Besides, they undergo practical training regarding these method subjects. the practical aspects of training consists of the activities of observation, demonstration and criticism of lessons. The student-teachers are required to take up one of the crafts such as agriculture, metal work, rural engineering etc. They are also required to undertake community life activities such as games and sports, debates, talks, music, mass literacy, social service, etc. Besides these, there are theoretical papers carrying hundred marks on history of education, educational psychology and guidance, school administration and health education. Thus, we see that the syllabus[10] of B.Ed. course is pretty lengthy and exhaustive. It is not practicable. The student-teacher is expected to achieve something which is not possible within a short period of 10 months. The duration of this training programme should be extended form ten months to 'two years'.[11]

The main objectives of Bachelor of Education Programme may be summed up as follows:

---

10. See, Appendix II.
11. As recommended by Mudaliar Commission in 1952-53.

1. It prepares better equipped teachers to accept the challenge of our country.
2. It prepares better equipped educationist, supervisors and administrators to rise equal to occasion.
3. It gives the trainees adequate knowledge of the theoretical and practical aspects of leading and learning process.

These aims and objectives are not at all realised, because it is not possible for a training college to achieve these ends during this short duration of ten months, and with the limited resources in hand. In the atmosphere of the training college, right from the practice of teaching skill to the activities motivating personal and professional growth, much artificiality prevails. Hardly any effect is carried over to the school when they join school as a teacher. It s also due to the non-realisation of the objectives set for training colleges that the skills imparted to trainees in these institutions have little bearing on the school practice.

As our concern here is exclusively with the problems of teaching English in training colleges of Bihar, we would like to examine them from different angles and dimensions.

First of all we must know that the student-teacher at this stage is required to achieve the following aims and objectives:

(i) to speak fluently so as to develop pupils' ability to understand English when spoken,

(ii) to differentiate between good speech from poor when English is spoken by his pupils, and to help them develop good and correct speaking ability.

(iii) to be able to read with proper stress, intonation, ease and enjoyment any material so as to enable pupils to read English effectively,

(iv) to be able to write correctly, and

(v) to be genuinely interested in language teaching.

The problems of teaching English in training colleges of Bihar are related to the problem of teaching English in schools. Until and unless good students turn up for getting training in these colleges, the fate of teaching and learning will remain pitiable in these colleges.

The student-teachers even after receiving training from these colleges are familiar neither with the teaching aids, nor with the effectiveness and limitations of these aids. The teachers here also do not keep themselves abreast of the modern developments and results of the researches in linguistics and language teaching.

The present syllabus of English methodology of the training colleges of Bihar have a number of drawbacks. They lay too much emphasis on the theoretical knowledge of various methods and techniques. They do not, however, lay emphasis on the practical application of this knowledge to specific problems. They fail to recognise the fact that the students' command of English is usually deficiency and that some provision needs to be made for remedying this deficiency. No doubt, they should know such theoretical topics like the role of English in various spheres of the Indian national life, but the student-teachers should also be given opportunity to improve their linguistic knowledge.

It will not be irrelevant if we see the scheme of examination and the place of English teaching in the B.Ed. course :

Paper		Subject	Hours	Marks
(A) Theoretical Examination				
(I)		Philosophy and Sociology in Education	3	100
(II)		Psychology in Education	3	100
(III)		Education in India (including Health Education)	3	100
(IV)	*(A)*	Methods subject I	3	100
	(B)	Methods subject II	3	100
		Total marks		500
(B) Practical Examination				
(V)		Practical Teaching		
		Methods subject I		100
		Methods subject II		100
		Total		200

(VI)	Work Experience	
(VII)	Extra-Mural Activities	
(VIII)	Sessional work on each of the two practical teaching subjects	200

After two months of getting instruction in theory papers, all the student-teachers are expected to teach their method subjects to the students of some specified schools. The training colleges believe that before the student-teachers take up actual classroom teaching, they should be made familiar with the principles of teaching. It takes time to decide the pace at which the class can work best. The student-teacher acts as an assistant to the regular teacher in the practice-teaching in schools. He looks up for assistance to the latter for all kinds of assurances and aspirations. He gains tremendously in this process. He learns to control and direct the children's behaviour as much as his own psychological activity. In the process of practice-teaching he acquires the powers of observation, attention, teaching imagination and a sense of time. He learns how to prepare his lessons independently.

Teaching during internship, criticism lessons and lesson planning form the major content of evaluation of skill in teaching. The training colleges evaluate the student-teacher's performance in class teaching on co-operative basis. It is done with the help of everyone concerned with the guidance and supervision of class teaching, *viz.* the college supervisors from the subject and the co-operating teachers/Headmasters/ Principals, etc.

The evaluation of the sessional work of the student-teacher is done by the subject department. The content of the sessional work evaluation constitutes three main items of activities (1) Observation of teaching (2) Preparation of teaching aids (3) Field experience. The subject departments require each student-teacher of their department to submit to them the following materials on the basis of which they assess the trainees' performance in sessional work and also form an idea of their attainment in skill in teaching. They are : lesson plan note books, supervision, note-books, written assignments, records of observation of lessons, teaching aids, etc.

But, now-a-days, in most of the training colleges of Bihar, this training programme has lost its value to a greater extent and the practical teaching has been reduced to a mere formality. Neither the student-teacher is interested to know more and more through experience nor the teacher of the method subject bothers to see whether trainees are doing their job seriously or not. So far as the teaching of English in these training colleges is concerned, it is hampered also owing to the lack of teachers. Each training college must have at least two teachers to teach English to the teacher-students of this particular methodology, but we came to know, to our great surprise, that some colleges do not have even a single teacher to teach English methodology. For example, we may take the case of Patna Women's Training College. Its English teacher retired in 1983, but up-till-now no teacher of English has been appointed. The single teacher of English at Patna Training College has also been engaging classes of English methodology in that college as well. Under such circumstances, it is very difficult to teach the essentials of the teaching methodology English syllabus. It is very difficult to supervise the practice teaching of student-teachers. To avoid this sad plight, appointment should be made prior to retirements at least, the process to fill the vacancy must start before time.

So far as government teachers training colleges are concerned, their condition too is very far from being satisfactory. There also they face the same problem. They face this problem also on account of the frequent transfer of expert teachers to administrative assignments. As these colleges are government colleges, teachers of English are, sometimes, deputed as District Education Officers somewhere or the other and, thus, teaching work of that college hampers for long time. To avoid this, alternative arrangements should be made before time to ensure smooth teaching.

The student-teacher finds himself at a loss owing to the lack of qualified teachers, and suitable textbooks. In spite of his zeal and dedication, he fails to devote himself to learning and teaching. The syllabus of B.Ed. Course, too, has grown outdated and it needs revision. The syllabus of English Method must include such topics as may enable the student-teachers to become efficient teachers. The student-teachers must be given some insight into the structures of the English language. They should know something about its sounds, its grammar and its vocabulary. All teaching calls for some kind of selection and some kind of organization. Words and constructions have to be selected on the basis of frequency, usefulness and teachability. The carefully selected language material constitutes the essence of good teaching. Student-teachers should also be made aware of the influence that the mother-tongue language habits exert on the learning of English.

The syllabus of English for training college must include the psychology of foreign language learning.

> The chief areas are memory, motivation, attention, interest and habit formation. Pupil-teachers need to know that a good lesson by the teacher does not by itself ensure good learning by the pupils. For proper learning, there must be an 'effort after meaning' on the part of the learners, and this effort must be renewed. The learner learns a word or construction after several meetings with it, in meaningful contexts. Controlled repetition is necessary for the establishment of language points. A through presentation of a teaching point on a single occasion does not often have the effect the teacher expects. Another important consideration is that of maintaining incentives or establishing a point once comprehension is achieved. This underlies the need for plenty of stimulating exercise materials in a language course.[12]

The importance of pronunciation in the teaching of English at this stage is very important, because the products of these training colleges will be entrusted with the job of teaching pronunciation to the Secondary School students. But this aspect remains completely neglected during training programmes. One of the reasons of its neglect may be the short duration of time. During the short period of ten months and at that, too, only two periods a week, it is not possible to cover all the aspects of teaching English. The periods for English classes must be raised from two to ten a week. This is possible if we have sufficient teacher to teach. During the training programme, the student-teachers must know English

12. The Study of English in India, p. 237.

vowels (including diphthongs); English consonants-plosive, affricate, nasal, fricative' semi-vowels; word stress, sentence stress and rhythm; strong and weak patterns of English language, and so on.

The student-teachers are expected to learn in these training colleges the use of blackboard and other audio-visual aids. During our survey, we found out that some teacher-students were not satisfied with the teaching which they received in these colleges during their training programme. They often put the blame on their teachers, saying that the training they were receiving from their teachers was theoretical and not practical. The English method teachers used to come and lecture for the whole period about the usefulness of blackboard and other visual aids but never tried to draw on the blackboard or other aids himself. It was also noticed that some of the method teachers were not conversant with the recent researches in the field of linguistics and language teaching. Therefore, the English method teachers themselves be able to draw on the blackboard, make visual aids and operate audio-visual machines. The teacher-students should in their turn acquire the practical skills of using the blackboard and other audio-visual aids efficiently. They should learn to design, make and use flash cards, matching cards and charts. They should also learn to operate simple audio-visual equipments. But the greatest problems is that we do not have such machines in our training colleges.

The present system of examination for B.Ed. Courses is also faculty. The questions asked are of repetitive nature and the teacher-students prepare only selected answer on the basis of bazaar notes. To cap it all, mass scale use of unfair means in the examination system makes it a veritable force. Until and unless a foolproof system is evolved and only serious and intelligent students are allowed to go for training, nothing worthwhile can be expected. A student-teacher who himself passes by using unfair means cannot be expected to set things right in the school when he becomes an actual teacher there. Therefore, the tests should be periodical and objective type of questions should be asked in the examinations. The importance and significance of periodical tests to verify progress should be brought home to these student-teachers. They should acquire proficiency in constructing test items for testing the pupil's knowledge of the elements of the English language. These student-teacher should be expected "to prepare and administer and score a test of 30 to 40 items on the practice lessons they give. Such a test should include items requiring long answers, multiple choice items and puzzles".[13]

One of the biggest problems of teaching English in training colleges is the low standard of proficiency in English among the trainees. The objectives of teaching and learning are defeated owing to their poor knowledge of English. The situation would have improved if only those candidates who took special English in degree cources had been allowed to take English method in the B.Ed. Courses. However, very few students having Honours in English seek admission to these training colleges. Therefore, there must be a content course in the B.Ed. syllabus. It will help in enhancing the proficiency in English of the student-teacher. Only good students can acquire a clear grasp of the usages, be they linguistic or literary. The student-teachers should also be made familiar with some suitable supplementary readers available in the market. It will enable them to develop in their pupils a taste for reading English books for profit and pleasure once they join schools as teachers.

But to cover all these of teaching English, all facilities should be provided to student-teachers and teachers of training colleges of our state. It is an open secret that some of the training college (like Government Teacher Training College, Gaya) do not even have adequate rooms and space to impart training to the student-teachers. It is also a fact that student-teachers do not take this programme seriously. They join training colleges because they have nothing to do. Therefore, such student-teachers can never be serious in their studies. Then, there are colleges which do not have good libraries and reading rooms for the trainees. The library occupies the central place in the programme of education.

13. The Study of English in India, p. 241.

It is an essential instrument for putting progressive educational methods into practice. In view of its crucial importance, each of these training colleges must be provided with a well-stocked library a permanent librarian and a comfortable reading room. There must be the provision of a period for training in the use of the library. As a teacher is the pivot around which all the activities of education revolve, maximum care must be taken of the preparation of teachers who can make teaching fair and cost-effective.

The teacher-students of these training colleges after passing their examinations teach English to the students of Secondary Schools, therefore, it is essential that competent teachers of English be prepared at these training colleges. And once we have accepted the three language formula, we teach English as a second language in our schools, and for its proper teaching a large number of good teachers are required. One of the reasons for the lower standard of English at secondary stage is the lack of teachers having good knowledge of English. So long as the standard of English continues to be low at this stage, there is bound to be the paucity of competent and efficient teachers in the schools. In order to improve the standard of English in schools, there should be the provision of meticulous training for teachers. They must be well-versed in the methodology of teaching, besides having a thorough knowledge of the subject itself.

The Institute of English located in the State Capital was set up in 1962 to trained and retrained English teachers. But this Institute has always been under-staffed and it is not fully equipped to early on the task of in-service training. It is unfortunate that whatever resources are available in the shape of staff-equipment, etc. are not fully utilised. Response from teachers to in-service training courses conducted by this Institute is not satisfactory and many teachers sponsored for training at this Institute do not turn up for training. It was also found out that most of the sponsored teachers were often above fifty years of age and they were not teaching English at their schools. It may, therefore, be said that teachers do not take this in-service training programme seriously. One of the reasons mentioned for this lack of response is the want of incentive for those who complete training. But incentive is not always essential. The government should see that all teachers of English should attend this training programme without fail. The syllabus[14] of this training course is certainly attractive and up-to-date, but a single teacher, within a period of four months of in-service training programme, is not sufficient to achieve the aims and objectives of this programme. Now this Institute has been merged with the State Council of Educational Research & Training, Patna, Bihar.

---

14. See Appendix II.

6 The Teaching of English Pronunciation

Pronunciation teaching is one of the most important as well as obtrusive aspects of English language teaching. Every teacher who teaches English by word of mouth is bound to pronounce it and to teach its pronunciation, consciously or unconsciously, to his students. The attitude adopted by the teacher towards the problem of pronunciation has its lasting impact on his students. Naturally, every teacher must adopt an attitude towards the problem of pronunciation. His attitude may not necessarily be positive; it may even be negative, allowing the students' pronunciation to take care of itself. The only circumstance where this problem can be ignored is the teaching of English through correspondence courses. It is true that the majority of people engaged in teaching English in India are themselves neither equipped nor qualified to teach pronunciation, and this is the reason why this aspect of English language teaching has remained neglected so far. John Haycraft describes this obsessive concern in the following words:

> Foreign teachers often lack confidence to teach it methodically and English teachers sometimes have a complex about it. As with English grammar, applied phonetics* is rarely taught in school or even university and therefore seems an alien, abstract subject....[1]

Peter Strevens puts forward a different reason for the neglect of pronunciation teaching. To him, the teachers of English as a second language neglect this aspect of the language because they do not find the learning of pronunciation proportionate to their teaching of pronunciation. As Strevens himself puts it :

---

* 'applied phonetics' here refers to pronunciation.

1. John Haycraft, *An Introduction to English Language Teaching* (London: Longman, 1978), p. 55.

> The problems of teaching pronunciation are often confused with the problems of learning pronunciation. It is sometimes difficult to be certain how far the learning is the result of the teaching: in the realm of pronunciation the inter-relations between learning and teaching are intricately entwined. Every word, every syllable, every phoneme uttered by the teacher may contribute to the learner's learning of pronunciation, not only when the teacher is deliberately and overtly concentrating on teaching pronunciation but equally when the teacher believes he is putting the weight of his vocabulary, or when he is simply easing the class along by an exchange of greetings or telling a little story.[2]

It appears that the teacher of English forgets the fact that the English spelling system is confusing and deficient in its power to show unambiguously the pronunciation that a word or sequence of words should have. This point is so well known that it does not require any illustration here. We do not even intend at this point to discuss reasons forth complexity of the English spelling system, or to suggest ways and means to make it easy. It is, however, worth mentioning here that no system of English spelling, howsoever systematic and scientific, will provide the foreign learners with sufficient information and insight to enable him to acquire native-like competence in all matters of pronunciation. There are, for example, certain features of English speech, such as its word-stress or neutral vowels in unstressed syllables, which can in no circumstances be transcribed in any orthography. The fact that any orthography of English, simple or complex, systematic or otherwise, will come up at a later stage in our discussion. These specific problems pertaining to the teaching of certain aspects of English orthography *vis-a-vis* its pronunciation apart, the learning of the pronunciation of any language cannot be proportionate to its teaching. It is because learning pronunciation involves both mental and physical activities, and physical deficiency, if any, cannot be cured by any amount of teaching. Strevens rightly says:

2. Peter Strevens, *New Orientations in Teaching of English* (Oxford : Oxford University Press, 1977), p. 80.

> Pronunciation is the sector of language where the organisation of syntax and semantics, having first been generated in the brain as a series of solely *mental* process—silent, instantaneous, electrical and chemical—is converted into *motor* activity, which in turn produces acoustic effect, *i.e.* audible sounds. The immensely delicate link between brain and muscles sets pronunciation apart from all other facets of language except writing. .... Any human action that are psycho-motor in nature, rather than solely mental are by definition subject to the limitations which apply to all muscular training. In a sense—though this is an oversimplification—teaching pronunciation is more like gymnastics than linguistics.[3]

It is true that the learning of pronunciation depends more on the student's own ability, mood, age and situation than on teaching, but that is no excuse for neglecting the teaching of pronunciation, 'rather it strengthens the plea that pronunciation should be taught and taught with more care and expertise than other aspects of the language'.[4] We do not find any point of disagreement with MacCarthy when, emphasizing the need for teaching of pronunciation, he says :

> .....the first point I want to make is that English pronunciation must be taught; the teacher should be prepared to devote some of the lesson time to this, and by his whole attitude to the subject should get the student to feel that here is a matter worthy of receiving his close attention. So, these should be occasions when other aspects of English, such as grammar, or spelling, are allowed for the moment to take second place.[5]

There is, therefore, no disputing the fact that the teaching of English pronunciation deserves special care and attention. Since the difficulties in learning to produce the sounds of English are mainly associated with the contrasts between the sound systems of the mother-tongue and those of English, the teacher should take note of the segmental and supraseg-

3. *Ibid.*
4. A.K. Sharma, *Aspects of English Language Teaching in India* (Bhagalpur : Bharat Book Depot, 1985), pp. 202-3.
5. P.A.D. MacCarthy, *Talking of Speaking : Papers in Applied Phonetics* (London : Oxford University Press, 1972), p. 14.

mental features which are liable to cause trouble. It is often found that Indians have trouble producing a particular English sound because our languages do not have that sound. No Indian language, for instance, has the exact equivalent of the first sounds of *thin* and *this*, consequently the speakers of Indian languages must learn these new sounds when they study English. Another factor which causes difficulty to the Indian students of English is the distribution of English phonemes. A glance at the distribution of English /S/ and /h/ phonemes may make this point clear. The phoneme /s/ occurs in the initial and ultimate positions of words, as in *such, some, sun, sit,* and *miss, kiss, less, pass, mass,* etc. It also occurs in consonental clusters in both of these positions, as in *sky, strip, straw, slight, spring, smash, snake,* and *gasp, mist, alms, sense, aesthetics, physics,* etc. The distribution of /h/, on the other hand, is comparatively more limited than that of /s/, for /h/ never ends an English word, or occurs in combination with any other consonant in the same word. An English speaker learning a language like Urdu or Persian, where /h/ occurs in the ultimate position of a word, finds it difficult to produce an acceptable sound even though English has a /h/ phoneme. The English speaker of Persian, for example, tends to omit the final /h/ sound when he pronounces the word *Shah* or *nikah*.

Though not an easy proposition, yet every teacher of English pronunciation must first build up a sequence of elements to be taught. As Broughton *et al.* put it:

> The teaching sequence must be organised in terms of priorities and degrees of difficulty. The amount of time devoted to specifically pronunciation teaching depends on the larger priorities of the course in general. A useful guide is the precept 'little and often'. The teacher should be prepared to slip a few minutes' pronunciation drill into a lesson at any point where a significant problem is noticed. But random assistance should not take the place of a systematic attempt to integrate pronunciation teaching into the course.[6]

6. G. Broughton, C. Brumfit R. Flavell, P. Bill and A. Pincas, *Teaching English as a Foreign Language* (London : Routledge and Kegan Paul, 1978), p.66.

This sequence will get automatically prepared once the teacher starts taking interest in the spoken language. What is required on the part of the teacher is the theoretical knowledge of phonetics and the will to apply that knowledge to the practical teaching of pronunciation. The teacher should not simply misuse his theoretical knowledge by taking for granted that his students are interested in the study of phonetics. A course in phonetics given by the teacher must automatically lead to the teaching of students to acquire a good pronunciation. It has been found during our survey that teachers do correct their students' errors in accordance with the accepted methods, and yet fail to apply those methods while teaching. There is, thus, a sort of lack of co-ordination between the errors committed by students and their diagnosis in phonetic terms by teachers.

Coming back to the proposition of preparing a sequence of elements for pronunciation teaching, the teacher ought to provide a corrective to restore the balance between possible distinctions and normal language use. The first point to be borne in mind in this connection is that a phonemic opposition that distinguishes between words under certain circumstances may not do so in others. For instance, the difference in English between /i:/ and /I/ allows us to keep separate two very large groups of words that might otherwise be confused : *feel/fill, peel/pill, keel/kill, meal/mill,* etc. In unstressed word-final position, however, the /i:/-/I/ difference is not maintained-native speakers of English may produce either vowel, or something in between, without causing any confusion as to what the word was intended to be : the final vowel of such words as *lovely, pity, infantry,* etc. does not have to be specified clearly as one or the other of the two phonemes. Similarly the pronouns *he* and *she* regularly occur with either /i:/ or /I/ when unstressed in the normal flow of connected speech. It would, therefore, be uncalled for, rather incorrect, in these instances, to insist on the students pronouncing a distinct version of one or the other phoneme. In fact, pronunciation and the maintaining of potential phonological opposition do not depend on a knowledge of the sound system alone: knowledge of vocabulary and syntax also plays a part in the process by which a native speaker pronounces a word. Given the construction the *fees are too high alread....*, there is only one thing that the missing vowel could be. It is predictable from the linguistic context, and also from the hearer's lexical knowledge of his language. The exact quality of the final vowel is therefore of no consequence; almost anything would do, and in practice speakers do produce a wide range of vowel qualities under such circumstances.

To take an example from the consonants, /m/ and /n/ would normally be treated by teachers as distinct phonemes, yet the distinction between them—the point of articulation—is completely obscured in normal conversation by the assimilation that takes place, for instance, before a labiodental, as in the words *configuration* [kədmfigjuciʃn] and *comport* (kʌmfʃt); or in connected speech : *Anyone for Patna* (əniwʌ nfəpatna). Instead of the bilabial or alveolar nasal, a third type, a labiodental nasal /m/, is produced, which cannot in any principled way be assigned to either of the two standard nasal phonemes. To insist that students make a clear distinction between the two when there is a following /f/ or /v/ is to insist on an unnatural pronunciation, one not made by native speakers.

To pursue this point a little further, many sounds that our students produce when they pronounce a word in isolation are obliterated when they pronounce the same word in normal connected speech, even though these sounds may carry important grammatical information. One of the most remarkable instances of this can be found in the case of the alveolar stops /d/ and /t/, which mark the "past simple" and "past participial" forms of most English Verbs. It commonly happens that these occur after a Verb-final consonant or consonant cluster, as in *laughed*/ laft/, *advanced* /ədvanst/, *practised*/ praktist/, *loved*/ Iʌʃd/, *moved*/ muvd/, etc. When the following words begin with a consonant, the /t/ or /d/ marking the grammatical distinction is regularly dropped in normal speech: *advanced method Stressed-vowel* /stress ?Vauəl/, *loved fishing*/Iʌ vfin/ *kept coming* /kep kʌ min/. The fact that the native speaker can omit /t/ and /d/ in these circumstances whows that the transmission of accurate meaning is in no way impaired as a result. Once again, it would be wrong and uncalled for to insist that our students pronounce these sounds, in spite of their grammatical role, because, although students would not actually be incorrect if they pronounced these sounds, they would of course be deviating form the normal practice of the native speakers of English, and would also often sound odd or pedantically over precise. Surely, what we aim at bringing our students to achieve is a native-like pronunciation.

That we strive to make our students adhere to the standard British English, *i.e.* Received Pronunciation (R.P.), is true, but what actually we have done with regard to pronunciation teaching is not far to seek. Our students speak their mother tongue in English, that is say, the speakers of Bhojpuri, Magahi, Maithily and Angika make use of the sounds of their respective languages when they speak English. What Gokak said in 1964 is true even today:

> But for a few schools in which the Received Standard is carefully drilled home to children, perhaps neglecting the teaching of other subjects somewhat in order to achieve this , the only standard that confronts us is the Regional Standard. Our pupils, and indeed many of their teachers, speak English as if it were Hindi, Bengali, Marathi or Tamil. Our regional speech habits have absorbed spoken English and regionalisted it. Spoken English is no longer used outside the English classroom in our schools and even in many of our colleges. One is not very sure how far it is used even during the English periods in schools. Many teachers fall back slyly on the translation and grammar method while teaching English, either because they are not convinced of the efficacy of the oral approach or are not equipped will enough to practise it. In colleges in which English is the medium of instruction, it has become increasingly difficult to hear grammatically correct English spoken, let alone the niceties of its spoken form.[7]

Not only this, majority of our students even after studying English for ten years or so find themselves unable to perform quite simple everyday transactions, *e.g.* make an arrangement, telephone people, state their identity without frequent breakdowns in communication. They cannot respond

7. V.K. Gokak, *op. cit.*, pp. 74-75.

adequately or appropriately even to simple and straightforward questions. Their utterances are at best slow and laboured and at worst only partly understood. They feel like prisoners of the language—forced to remain silent when they could make a perfectly valid point and trapped into expressing themselves in ways which do not reflect what they think. They are not able to follow lectures and participate in group discussions. They do not know how to behave in the language, that is, how and when to criticise, to apologise, or to make suggestions, and this makes them feel ill-at-ease.

The problem, as we have perceived it, is that majority of students have difficulty with English stress-timed rhythm, with vowel length and with lexical stress. There are, too, the usual crop of vowel and consonant problems which lead them to adopt a slow, deliberate, formal style of pronunciation, frequently marked by strong interference. They have, then, very limited experience in using English to communicate, for their English has been limited to the closely contextualized and highly predictable language of the classroom. They do not appear to have ever expressed what they feel or think. They are also weak particularly in matching spoken performance to whatever underlying language-competence they possess. When put under pressure, they go on making 'unnecessary' mistakes or agonising over what phonological and grammatical rules they should employ while speaking. Lastly, most of the students see the problem as one of good teaching in the classroom alone rather than efficient learning in the total language environment, *i.e.*, learning through conversation, through listening to tapes, radio and television. They are reluctant to take responsibility for their improvement even when the appropriate strategies for doing so have been spelt out.

This is the situation in which a teacher of English is supposed to teach pronunciation. "The result", says Gokak, "is that intelligibility has begun to suffer even in our interprovincial contact. The typical Tamilian and Assamese do not easily understand each other when they converse in English..... The point at issue is.... that our methods of teaching a second language. We teach it as if it were a dead language.

We teach it as if it would be adequate for a student to recognise a word in the language by it spelling".[8]

He find it ' fantastic that a living language which has to be used for several important purposes in its spoken from and, which we have agreed should be taught through the oral approach, should be allowed to be spoken by thousands of students as if it were Bengali, Kannada or Gujarati. It is high time we amended our ways in this regard'.[9]

By way of amending our ways in this regard, we will have to decide the target model of pronunciation to be taught in the schools and colleges of India in general and Bihar in particular. Indian scholars of English have made much fuss about the selection of the variety or accent of English to be taught in our classrooms. David Abercrombie feels it unnecessary for most language learners to acquire a perfect pronunciation. According to him, in place of a normally unrealized ideal of perfection, pronunciation teaching should have 'a limited purpose which will be completely fulfilled; the attainment of intelligibility'.[10]

It is true that Received Pronunciation is a 'regionally neutral' variety of English, but its adoption as a teaching model in Bihar under the aforesaid circumstances does not seem possible. To quote Abercrombie:

> It is true that Received Pronunciation is socially the most advantageous of the dialects of England when used in that country : but outside England, in the rest of the English-speaking world (including Scotland), it carries with it no special privileges, though it is, of course, widely understood. There are, moreover, other forms of English which in England itself rank socially equal with Received Pronunciation—Scottish, Irish and American, for example. For the foreigner the great drawback of Received Pronunciation is that it is equipped with a peculiarly difficulty set of vowel sounds: and in view of the fact that many foreigners who learn English intend to use it

8. *Ibid.*, p. 75.
9. *Ibid.*, pp. 75-76.
10. David Abercrombie, "Teaching Pronunciation", in *English Language Teaching III*, 5 (February, 1949), pp. 120-21.

elsewhere than in England, and that number of English teachers abroad do not teach Received Pronunciation (for it is not by any means the accent of all educated Englishmen), I believe, here is a case to be made out against basing a 'limited goal' programme of pronunciation teaching on this particular style. There is certainly room for experiment both in teaching other accents, and in exploring the potentialities of a 'synthetic style' of speech as a basis.[11]

There is no reason in not being in complete agreement with what Mr. Abercrombie says. The adoption of R.P. as a target model for teaching pronunciation in Bihar is a thoroughly unrealistic proposition. The attainment of that model will be an ideal, but the question is how to attain that. Not even one per cent of the teachers of English in Bihar speak that accent. Who will teach that and make students practise that in a situation where there is absolutely no exposure to that accent? Once we decide to adopt R.P. speaking personnel and appoint them in our schools and colleges for this very purpose, which, needless to say, would be much too expensive. Even if it is done, our students have not to learn pronunciation alone, but a large number of things. This accent can be taught and students can be made to practise it, but at the cost of their learning of other subjects.

The other aspect of the proposition is that these students will have no exposure to this accent outside their classrooms, nor will each one of them afford to have the cassette tapes having the materials for teaching R.P. accent recorded on them. Socially prestigious is this variety of English, and it does earn a sort of distinction for its speakers, but in our society such a speaker becomes the odd man out, finding it difficult to fit himself into the community of which he is a member. He becomes a laughing stock, as people make caricature of his voice in his absence, stressing the features and mannerisms of his accent in order to cause ridicule. This may be the reason why some of the teachers, who had acquired

---

11. David Abercrombie, *Problems and Principles : Studies in the Teaching of English as a Second Language* (London : Longmans Green & Co., 1957), pp. 39-40.

this accent during their long stay in England and spoke it quite competently even on their return to India, now feel shy of speaking English with an R.P. accent.

Let us look at the question of selecting a target model for teaching English pronunciation from another angle. In countries outside England where English is spoken by a vast majority or people, they do not go in for the R.P. accent. We know of the American, Scottish, Irish, Canadian and Australian accents. In England itself, we know of dialects, such as, Western, Northern, Central, etc., which are as popular as the R.P. itself. If, at all, we too have a choice, we may go in for an accent which would be widely acceptable in India and abroad, for it will be used in both national an international communication. The typical Indian pronunciation of English, it is true, suffers in intelligibility. What Perer Strevens says about African pronunciation of English is completely applicable to ours as well :

> In the first place it contains a smaller number of vowels and diphthongs than do other pronunciations....Secondly, it does not make a distinction made in most other dialects of English, the distinction of vowel-length, by which the vowels in words like *heed, hard, pool,* are no longer than the vowels in *hid, had, pull.* Thirdly, all syllables of energy, unlike other dialects of English, in which there is a great difference made between 'stressed' (strong) and unstressed (week) syllables. Finally, it does not contain a system of intonation, at any rate of the same kind as that found in almost every other dialect of English.[12]

These, according to Strevens, are the reason why African pronunciation suffers in intelligibility, and these, more or less, are the reasons why the English pronunciation of the average Indians too suffers in intelligibility. In the case of Africa, pronunciation of English, which is in between the Africans' original pronunciation and that of the Englishman, is the only solution to remedy the situation and to make the African speakers of English realize the inadequacy of the average African pronunciation. The well-educated Africans, however,

---

12. Peter Strevens, *Spoken Language* (London: Longmans Green and Co., 1956), p. 30.

"acquire a form of speech that quite definitely qualifies for inclusion in the list of 'educated ' pronunciations",[13] and the highly educated ones "acquire a pronunciation of English indistinguishable from that of an Englishman".[14] Pointing out the difference between the Educated African pronunciation and the general African pronunciation, Strevens further observes :

> It contains a large number of vowels, diphthongs and consonants, it contains a stress-system, and it contains a system of intonation. It corresponds exactly to Educated Canadian or Australian......in that it is clearly identified with an area of the world, Africa, but is completely intelligible to speakers of other educated dialects (*i.e.* R.P., American Standard, etc.). Finally, it is intelligible to the speakers of the local dialects of English in Africa (*i.e.* those who use average African pronunciation).[15]

If Educated African English is intelligible in both national and international communication, so is Educated Indian English, and we find no reason why this should not be our target model for teaching English pronunciation in the schools and colleges of Bihar. We should go in for what is both intelligible an attainable and not pine for what cannot at any cost be attained. Scholars like V.K. Gokak[16], R.K. Bansal[17], P.B. Pandit[18], P. Nihalani, R.K. Tongue, P. Hosali[19] and A.K. Sharma[20] have rightly argued for the adoption of Education Indian English *for* teaching English pronunciation in India.

What E.V. Gatenby has observed in this connection should be the eye opener for the teachers and scholars of English in India. He says :

---

13. *Ibid.*, p. 34.
14. *Ibid.*
15. *Ibid.*, pp. 34-35.
16. V.K. Gokak, *op. cit.*
17. R.K. Bansal, *The Intelligibility of Indian English* (C.I.E., Monograph no.4, 1969).
18. P.B. Pandit, "Indian Readjustments in the English Consonant System", in *Indian Linguistics 25.*
19. P.B. Nihalani, R.K. Tongue and P. Hosali, *Indian and British English: A Handbook of Usage and Pronunciation* (Delhi: OUP, 1979).
20. A.K. Sharma, *op. cit.*

> There are many varieties of English—Canadian, Welsh, Scotch, Australian, Irish, American, etc.—and any mutually intelligible form of educated English is universally acceptable. Indian English exists. It is as worthy of acceptance as any other brand of English, and the time has come for this establishment as a Regional Standard. Professor Fries has indicated by his phonetic system what the sounds and speech habits of educated Middle West American English in general use are, and similar work to discover what the 'received' standard in India is would be the first step to furnish Indian English with the authority it needs. Seetting up such a regional standard would save a good deal of time in teaching and learning the language.[21]

We in India have had a long debate over the issue of a target model of spoken English for teaching purposes, and it is high time now that we stop making unnecessary fuss of the question of the selection of a model. Let Educated Indian English be our model and let us try to describe and document it and subsequently standardize it, so that it may be more acceptable and intelligible to people in both India and abroad. This variety of English is 'free from provincialism or the gravitational pull of the mother tongue, except for a few traces. It contains a larger number of vowels, diphthongs and consonants than the average Indian pronunciation of English. It has a stress-system and also a system of intonation.

It will not be out of place here to point out the differences between the vowel and consonant systems of Received Pronunciation and Educated Indian English. Let us first examine the vowel systems of the two varieties of English. These differences have been described by P. Nihalani, R.K. Tongue and P. Hosali which is as follows:

(i) Educated Indian English has two monophthong /e:/ and /o:/ in place of the diphthongs /eI/ and /o:/ in BRP.

	BRP	*EIE*
Coat	/Kəvt/	/Ko:t/
day	/deI/	/de:/

21. Quoted in V.K. Gokak, *op. cit.*, p. 80.

EIE speakers should be careful to add adequate length to both monophthong.

(ii) The central vowels / , /3:/ and /∂/ of BRP have only one corresponding vowel /∂/ in EIE.

	BRP	*EIE*
bud	/b d/	/b d/
bird	/b 3:d/	/b r d/
about	/∂bavt/	/∂bvt/

(iii) BRP vowels /b/ and /∂:/ have only one corresponding vowel /b/ in EIE.

	BRP	*EIE*
Cot	/kbt/	/'K∂t/
Caught	/K∂:t/	/Kb:t/

(iv) EIE is a rhotic accent, that is to say 'r' is pronounced wherever it occurs, unlike BRP where post-vocalic 'r' is not pronounced.

	BRP	EIE
cart	/Ka:t/	/Ka:rt/
air	/ε∂ /	/e∂r/
mother	/mvf∂/	/m∂dr/

(v) In BRP, the neutral vowel / / never occurs in a stressed syllable, whereas in EIE it does.

mother /m∂d∂r/[22]

Similarly, the differences between the consonant systems of BRP and EIE have been pointed out by them in the following words:

EIE differs from BRP in respect of the following :

(i) /V/ and /W/ are often replaced by one sound /v/ in EIE. The phoneme /V/ is realized as a frictionless labio-dental (articulated with the lower lip against the upper teeth) /v/ or weakly rounded /w/. The distinction between the two sounds /V/ and /W/ is very important in English and carries a high functional load; that is to say, there are a large number of words in English, which

22. P. Nihalani, R.K. Tongue, and P. Hosali, *op. cit.*, p. 211.

are different in meaning just because of this difference in sound. For example:

Vine	Wine
Vale	Whale
Vet	Wet

Indian learners have to acquire these two sounds in their speech and make them a part of their consonant inventory.

(ii) The alveolar sounds /t, d/ or BRP are sometimes retroflexed, *i.e.* articulated with the tip of the tongue curled back. This retroflexion increases the further south we travel in India. This gives our speech one of its chief Indian characteristics, and marks us immediately as foreign speakers of English, but it does not affect intelligibility.

(iii) /t, dn, ʃ , ɛ/ are articulated with the tongue tip down. In the production of /tʃ,dn, ʃ, n/, it is the blade of the tongue making an alveolar or post-alveolar contact. In BRP, it is the tip and not the blade. This affects intelligibility hardly at all. It might be helpful if Indian learners added some lip-rounding as a sort of secondary articulation.

(iv) /ʒ/ does not occur in the English of the majority of Indian speakers. As a result, the distinction between the voiceless palato-alveolar /ʃ/ and its voiced counterpart /ʒ/ is lost. The voiced form /ʒ/ is generally realized as voiceless /ʃ/. Even in British English, we *rarely* come across a minimal pair of English words where this distinction is maintained. Generally, it is in the borrowed (French words that (ʒ) is found, and so this sound does not carry a high functional load even in the phonological system of BRP. An EIE speakers loses nothing by dropping this distinction and so it need not constitute a learning item for EIE speakers.

(v) The affricates /θ,*f*/ are replaced by plosives / *th,d*/ in EIE. As long as this substitution is maintained *consistently* in the phonological system of EIE, there is nothing wrong with it except that it will render out speech typically Indian.

On the basis of the differences between the vowel and consonant systems of the British Received Pronunciation and Educated Indian English as pointed out by the aforesaid authors, it can be claimed that Educated Indian English cannot suffer in intelligibility in international communication, for it differs only marginally from British Received Pronunciation at the level of segmental phonemes. Students in the Schools and colleges of Bihar should be given a regular course in English pronunciation and that, we are sure, will enable them to pronounce English sounds well.

The problem of intelligibility, however, depends more on the supra-segmental features of the language, such as stress, rhythm and intonation, than on the segmental phonemes. The native varieties of English may differ on the segmental plane, but they have the same supra-segmental features characteristic to all the dialects. Indian learners of English, therefore, ought to acquire the stress system and rhythmic and intonational patterns of the British Received Pronunciation. Emphasizing the importance of stress, rhythm and intonation for the intelligibility of a spoken language, W.S. Allen observes:

> However accurately we learn to pronounce the isolated sounds of a language, we must still train ourselves to set them in motion in the right manner if we wish to make ourselves easily understood....a reasonably correct speech-flow is more important for intelligibility than correct sounds. It is possible to carry on an intelligible English conversation in a series of mumbles and grunts provided the voice movement is correct.......Some foreign speakers of English, even though they learn to make English sounds quite well, fail to acquire a sufficiently accurate speech-flow. The result is that English-speaking people find it quite difficult to understand them.[23]

R.K. Bansal has also dwelt upon and expressed his concern over the problem of a uniform standard of the pronunciation of the English in India. The suggestions he has made with regard to the measures to be adopted and practised while teaching English pronunciation in India are worth quoting:

23. W.S. Allen, *Living English Speech* (London: Longman Group Ltd., 1954), pp. XI-XII.

The standard of pronunciation should be based on accepted Indian uses, modified in the direction of native English to attain international intelligibility. The suggested modifications are:

(i) Correct patterns of accent and rhythm in words and sentences.

(ii) Division of longer sentences into proper groups.

(iii) Correct location of the intonation nucleus (tonic syllable).

(iv) Correct distribution of vowels and consonants.

(v) Vowels:

(a) Waking of vowels in unaccented syllables.

(b) /e/ in words like *made* should be given adequate length or made a diphthong /e:/ or /eI

(c) /D/ should be made long in words like *brought, exhaust, talk,* and /r/ should be retained after /o/ in words like *form* or *short.*

(vi) Consonants:

(a) /v,θ, f, w/ should be aspired.

(b) /p, t, k/ should be aspired at the beginning of accented syllables.[24]

The modifications suggested by R.K. Bansal are undoubtedly sure to add to the intelligibility of Indian English and make it a more prestigious variety of English than it is today. This variety of English, which is gaining ground day by day, is a synthetic style of speech which has its roots India and yet conforms to the phonological essentials of Standard English.' As P. Nihalani and his collaborators put it:

> Educated Indian English is a perfectly natural, and theoretically sound answer to the needs of Indian learners, whose number runs into millions.
>
> *(i)* This model will be well within the reach of Indian learners under normal school and college conditions.
>
> *(ii)* The task of training teachers in the use of this model will be much easier.

24. R.K. Bansal, *Introductions of English Language Teaching : Volume 2, Phonetics and Spoken English* (Delhi: OUP, 1978), pp.73-74.

(iii) This model will not encounter any psychological barriers such as fear of sounding foreign and lack of motivations.[25]

The last and most important aspect of pronunciation teaching is the selection of proper methods and techniques for presenting segmental and supra-segmental phonemes of English to the students in the schools and colleges of Bihar. There are methods which can be employed to teach pronunciation at the elementary level. Similarly, there are methods which can be used at the intermediate and advanced levels. Imitation and exhortation, for instance, are the methods one can employ in pronunciation teaching at the elementary state. Phonetic games and exercises based on certain sound features or contrasted may be useful at the intermediate stage. Advanced techniques of pronunciation teaching, such as the use of phonetic transcription, articulation diagrams, ear training, etc.; are to be employed at the advanced level of teaching alone.[26]

In order to achieve a higher standard of performance, the teacher should give factual information and point out what needs attention. He should select, grade and demonstrate whatever has to be presented to the students. The demonstration as to how a piece of pronunciation is to be done and how it is not to be done can be more effective. The teacher should put into execution techniques and procedures for getting effective results. When demonstrating at the elementary stages, the teacher must slow up the normal rate of utterance so that the student can catch the sound and grasp some point before having to cope with more rapid rates and longer stretches of speech. The teacher must present a good model of pronunciation to his students, and prepare them to be on the look-out for specific things, *i.e.* to be able to identify at once and with precision what they hear. What the teacher should try to get right is the articulation of English vowels and consonants, and the handling of the main features of sounds in sequence and connected speech. As Wilkins puts it:

Learning a pronunciation system is learning to operate a

25. P. Nihalani, R.K. Tongue and P. Hosali, *op. cit.*, p. 208.
26. See, Peter Strevens, *New Orientations in Teaching of English*, p. 65.

set of contrasts, and this can only be done if the practice itself gives the pupil the opportunity to relate phonemes to one another. As an isolated unit a phoneme has no phonetic form. We can only know how it is realize phonetically when we know its position and phonetic environment........ . The most systematic approach to pronunciation teaching reflects the procedures of phonemic analysis very closely and is the products of them.[27]

Now that once we decide to teach pronunciation and not to leave it to take care of itself, it is definitely a time-taking affair, and this, again, should not be made an excuse for not teaching it, rather the time at disposal should be used efficiently. In the average English language teaching/learning situation, with every aspect demanding attention, naturally pronunciation teaching competes with the rest for time, and to claim for it more than a fair share would be unrealistic. It is now upto the teacher to decide what should be the proper share for pronunciation teaching, taking everything into account.

It may be pointed out, by way of suggestion, that sounds and their patterns ought to be repeated over and over again before they really sink in, and many more times until they are really learnt. Repetition must be accepted as necessary to the learning process, especially where auditory phenomena are concerned. It should not be forgotten that the sounds of English are superimposed on those of the mother-tongue, which are already there in the mind and can hardly be obliterated. Every student is conditioned by his mother-tongue experience to react in terms of its specific phonological structure. This, naturally, creates problems as soon as he is required to react differently when confronted with the different phonological structure of the English language. Mother-tongue interference is evident at every level, not only at phonetic and phonological levels but syntactic and semantic as well. Systematic de-conditioning and training of the ear are the ways to lessen the interference of the phonological system of the mother-tongue. The teacher's role in this connection should be to provide students with the

---

27. D.A. Wilkins, *Linguistics in Language Teaching.*

opportunity to have practice at doing it. He must direct the attention of his students, with adequately clear demonstration, to the exact item to be learnt, giving them sufficient opportunities of listening for that specific item. Needless to say, this will enables each student to exercise his personal judgment on the supply the correct answer so that each student may check at once whether his judgment was correct or not.

In schools, particularly, the students in their respective classes can be given some practice by taking each in rapid alternation and getting each to articulate one or more times a given sound or syllable or a given word or phrse. The teacher should then make comments on their individual efforts, in particular letting them know individually when they have done something exactly right. This, we feel, is the way to lay the foundation of conscious control over one's own articulatory movements and also to make a beginning with the important next stage of new habit forming.

By way of summing up, it may be said that the best method of teaching pronunciation is one which works. It is, again, not the method that works, rather it is the teacher who makes a method work. The following passage from M.A.K. Haliday, A. MacIntosh and Peter Strevens is worth quoting in this connection:

> There are many devoted and brilliant teachers of English who lift their subject to the high level it should always occupy and provide vital, exciting instruction that illuminates languages and literature for their pupils in a deep and lasting way......There is more to this than the statistical observation that there will always be a proportion of teachers whose misfortune it is to make their subject dull and boring; the quantity of lifeless teaching in English seems to be greater than would be expected from the more random distribution of less inspiring teachers among subjects as a whole.[28]

As the pronunciation of English is to be learnt and not acquired by students in the schools and colleges of India, its

---

28. M.A.K. Halliday, A. MacIntosh and Peter Strevens, *op.cit.*, p. 273.

teaching must be done with meticulous care. It is also one of the most arduous and obtrusive aspects of English language teaching, hence it has got to bethought in a lively manner so that students do not get bored. One of the best ways of teaching it, therefore, can be to do it while seeming to be doing something else, and with this end in view, the teacher may make use of word-association drills, appropriate-response drills, question-and-answer drills, contradiction drills, deduction drills, etc.[29] These drills are sure to yield expected results and, at the same time, make the teaching of pronunciation lively and exciting.

---

29. See, Thomas J. Kral," Teaching Pronunciation (White seeming to be Doing Something Else)", in *English Teaching Forum Volume XVIII Number 2* (April 1980).

7 Conclusion

We have discussed in the foregoing chapters the position of English in India and the problems of its teaching/learning in the schools and colleges of Bihar. We shall, now, try to suggest some ways and measures which may help in resolving these problems. Due to historical reasons, English has become an integral part of our education system and its teaching/learning as a second language in our schools and colleges is likely to continue for many years to come. When we say English as a second language, we are reminded of a controversy regarding English—whether it is a second language or a third language in our school curriculum, but we use English as a second language. Moreover, the methodology of teaching a second language is very much applicable to the teaching of a third language as well. We need not, therefore, revise our aims and methods of teaching English.

It is true that the past three decades have seen a gradual lowering of the standard of English. We have discussed in the preceding chapters the reasons for this sharp deterioration in the standard of teaching/learning English in Bihar.

One of the important reasons for this sad state of affairs is socio-political problems of teaching English in Bihar. The vacillation in policy of the State Government with regard to the status of English must stop and a clear cut policy ought to be evolved for the creation of a proper situation for teaching and learning of English in Bihar.

In learning English, the role of motivation as an important factor cannot be denied. As most of the students in the schools and colleges of Bihar do not need to communicate in English, they lack proficiency in spoken English. To acquire proficiency in English, the learner must be exposed to language for a longer period of time. But very few students in Bihar do speak in

English to their parents, brothers, sisters, classmates and teachers. Under such circumstances it is very difficult for the teachers of English to create a proper English learning/teaching situation. The students of English in the schools and colleges of Bihar must be made to employ a wide variety of strategies, demonstrating their active involvement in learning. They should be made to repeat silently to themselves the sound they hear from the teachers or other sources of learning, such as radio, television etc. they must be made to participate sincerely in the activities of the classroom and take opportunities to discuss the lesson material with other students. Outside the classroom, they must be made to exploit every opportunity to use the language as a means of communication, for example, by seeking personal contacts, listening to the radio/television or reading newspapers.

For the proper teaching of English in Bihar a statement of the aims and objectives is essential. We have discussed in detail what should be our aims and objectives of teaching English to the students of school and colleges of Bihar. But one thing we want to emphasize is this that our aims and objectives should not be only grand and lofty. Our objectives should be realistic, need-based and goal oriented. The material for teaching English should reflect the special needs of the learners of different groups, areas and speech communities. The content of English language teaching should be the samples of the actual use of language. Special care should be taken of the areas where English is not the part of environment and where learners get absolutely no exposure to the language. The teacher should have full awareness of the situation in which language is to be taught. Central to the situations are the learners themselves. Diagnosis of their strength and weaknesses, their abilities and interests and their approach to learning will indicate to the teacher many suitable objectives for the learners to pursue. The language teachers must know the objectives expressed in specific terms. These objectives, then, can be used to plan language learning opportunities of the students and to devise means of assessing the extent to which the students have achieved those objectives.

Curriculum planning and course design are an essential pre-requisite for language teaching. The curriculum outlines the guiding principles on which the actual imparting of instruction is based. Planning curriculum for the teaching of English as a second language is not an easy affair. It requires a lot of caution and experience and insight on the part of those who are entrusted with this job. The first thing to be taken into consideration at the time of planning a curriculum for English as a second language course is to determine the basis of prescribing language materials for the students. The basis of a curriculum usually speaking, is to be sought in the objectives of English learning and teaching. Another problem which a curriculum planner is likely to face is that there are quite a number of competing descriptions of language written from different theoretical viewpoints. In our opinion, however, the curriculum planners should choose what is useful from different theoretical descriptions and pay no attention to what is irrelevant or impractical for his purpose. Some language in traditional grammars, others become clearer if they are looked at from a structural or a transformational point of view. A study of recent development in different branches of linguistics is useful because it gives us a choice of ways in which the difficulties of students can be approached and perhaps explained.

There are circumstances, however, which are quite beyond the control of the teacher. The syllabus itself, for example, is usually not within the control of ordinary teachers. Some older courses follow a 'linear' progression from one teaching point to the other. After the first point is taught quite exhaustively, the class moves on, without looking backward, to the next point and so on. The difficulty is that once a topic is finished, it is only incidentally referred to and practised later, resulting in poor learning on the part of students. Many course, of course, take care to build in the regular repetition of lexical and structural material, thereby reinforcing the original learning and increasing the students' exposure to it in new context. The 'spiral syllabus' has been said to be a means of ensuring that good teaching and effective learning achieve the right results. The idea here is that only one or two aspects of a teaching point are introduced and practised before moving on to another point. But the teaching plan comes back round to the first point fairly shortly and original structures are reinforced and extended.

Firstly, a syllabus must state its content in clear terms. Content might be described in terms of knowledge, skills, attitudes, values etc. to be learnt. Secondly, the syllabus must be specific both in its content and requirements. The syllabus for the teaching of English at any stage for instance cannot be framed in isolation from the stages preceding and succeeding. The target selected should be in keeping with the targets of the earlier stage. The third important point about a syllabus is that it must justify its objectives. The requirements specified in the syllabus must be amply justified in the light of the needs of the leaders in a given situation.

The design of the course, to begin with, must be based on principles of control, co-ordination, consolidation and correlation, control implies that whatever goes into the making of a language course should be subjected to a number of controls, *e.g.* linguistic, cultural, psychological and so on. Co-ordination relates to the fact that each part of a language learning programme extending over a period of time, and phased into stages, must be visualized in relation to the total programme, and not in isolation form the other stages. The third principle, *i.e.* consolidation relates to the consideration of blending the 'old' material with the 'new'. It will be relevant, for example, at the college level to revise language items learnt in school. The last principle, *i.e.* correlation implies that all the elements of a language programme should, at any given stage, be brought together and taken up simultaneously according to a plan.

The textbook may be described as the centre of instruction and, therefore, textbooks should be made an effective means to learning English efficiently and with ease. It should be the task of the teacher to direct the study of textbooks to the maximum linguistic advantage of the students. The value of a textbook lies primarily in its being of general appeal and interest to students and teachers alike. In order to enhance its usefulness and effectiveness, every textbook must be accompanied with a teachers book and a work-book, the former containing guidelines for the teachers and the latter containing exercises in primary, secondary and advanced skills for the students. Needless to say, a large number of textbooks being used for the teaching of English in the schools and college do obviously appear to have written to serve the mercenary ends of their writers rather than to meet the linguistic requirements of the students. They do not help in accelerating the process of learning/teaching. At University stage, too, books containing common vocabulary and common themes are more useful. As students are greatly handicapped in the power of self-expression, great emphasis should be laid on language course which consist of essay, letter writing, précis writing, grammar and syntax.

The programme of teaching English as second language can be implemented well by efficient methods and techniques. Of course, teachers with less professional competence cannot do justice with good methods and techniques. But this does not minimise the need of good methods and sound techniques. A good teacher of English must know what are good methods of teaching. Here we are not going to give a list of all the methods of teaching English as a second language, but we would like to point out what constitute a good method. A language teaching method must include the principles of selection, gradation, presentation and repetition. They help us to decide what to teach.

The selection of teaching items is essential, because 'no method can teach the whole of a language'. The whole of a language cannot be learnt all at once or haphazardly. A method of the selection of learnable language items has got to be adopted. Hence, selection is inherent in any learning/teaching activity. With the native speakers, the selection of speech items is automatic. He selects words as he needs them. He uses the sentence patterns as he chooses, but this is not the case with second language learners. The cardinal issues involved in the selection of a method are purpose, level and duration which affect the type and the amount to be selected. The items need to be selected in the light of general purposes or a certain specific purpose. The selection may be made for children or adolescents or adults. The level of proficiency of the learner should also be taken into consideration while selecting teaching materials. Similarly the duration of the language course is an important factor for selection of teaching items. A course may be for a few weeks only or for a few months or a year or two. The purpose, level and duration of the course affect the selection of the dialect, register, style and media to be included and taught.

Again, a number of criteria usually help in the selection of teaching items. These are *(i)* frequency, *(ii)* range, *(iii)* availability, *(iv)* coverage, *(v)* learnability. Items that are found occurring frequently in use-both in speech and writing are given priority to others. The use of the item in varieties of samples or texts, rather than only one, determines its 'range'. Certain items are more used in certain situations than in others. They are more available to convey meaning pertaining to specific situations. Some items have the 'covering' capacity of a number of things or meanings, *e.g.* an expression of gratitude in saying 'thank you' can be conveyed through several patterns. Some items are selected by virtue of their qualities like clarity, simplicity and preciseness in expression.

Next comes gradation of teaching items. The first stage of the language teaching process is the selection of language to be taught and, therefore, has no connection with the methods of teaching it. Gradation is the ordering of this selected language material for the purpose of a particular course along the dimensions of relative difficulty and relative usefulness. Selection of language items may be very studiously and meticulously made but more essential is the consideration of teaching ease. The teacher finds some meaning and joy in his teaching when he arranges or grades his items on order and prefers to teach materials that are useful, simple and teachable. The second principle of gradation is relative usefulness. Materials that are selected and graded are *(i)* structures sentence—structures, clause and phrase patterns formulas *(ii)* words—content words and structure words. The basic principles of gradation is to arrange the selected material in such a way that the less difficult and the more useful items come before the more difficult and less useful ones. Relative usefulness relates to purpose and duration of the course, whereas relative difficulty relates to the learners.

After selection and gradation of teaching items, our task is to teach them to the students. Presentation is teaching in a classroom situation. It means communicating something to somebody. It is for the sake of presentation that selection and gradation are done. Language teaching involves the presentation of *(i)* Form or Expression and *(ii)* Meaning or Content. The forms of language can be introduced to the students by its demonstration. It is through demonstration that the students are introduced to the written and spoken form of language. The process of demonstration at the intermediate and advanced stages should lead to the identification and production in spoken and written forms of words, sentences, stress and intonation, styles and registers etc. with fluency and ease. So far as the communication of the meaning of a second language is concerned, different procedures can be adopted for this purpose. The most important are differential procedures, ostensive procedures, pictorial procedures. Differential procedures can be adopted by those who allow the use of mother-tongue in teaching a second language. Translation is a patent device in the differential procedures. Ostensive procedures relate to the teaching of a second language through objects, actions and situations. Objects, for instance, can be used to teach *(a)* names of things like shirt, pants, bag, box, pen, pencil, chair, table *(b)* modifiers like big, small, long, short, much, many less, green, black etc. *(c)* abstract words like food, dress, metal etc. and *(d)* structure words like in, on, under, with etc. Meaning can also be taught through actions and gestures. One can, for instance, teach verbs like go, come, eat, drink, laugh, weeping, fall, rise, give, take, sleep, break, beat and so many of them through actions. Pictorial procedures are like ostensive procedures. The main difference is that pictures are fixed whereas object, actions and situations are moving. The contextual procedures aims at presenting real life through its linguistic manifestations and takes the situation itself as its basis. The second language should always be taught in contextualized form.

All these procedures can be of great use if they are used properly. Through these procedures, meaning can be both presented and drilled. But they need repetition because repetition is the last aspect of the language teaching process.

The importance of evolution in the teaching of English as a second language cannot be denied. It is an integral part of the teaching process. The measurement of achievement of the student is done through tests and examinations. We have discussed the system of examination and evaluation prevalent in Bihar in the preceding chapters. The traditional system of examination has many loopholes and it does not test the knowledge of the student. Generally examination are held at the end of an academic session and as the questions are of subjective nature, it encourages mechanical memorization of answers. There has been a marked change in methods and in concepts of what an examination or text might be expected to measure. So too we are now aware of the possible effects of a syllabus based examination and of the form of the examination itself upon the content and method of the course which prepares students for it. Much of the criticism levelled at tests and examination of all kind arises from the observation that they tend to stress unduly one particular objective—a command of vocabulary, of accurate grammatical or syntactic usage etc. Sometimes indeed the apparent case with which certain aspects of language learning can be tested—such as vocabulary in the form of word recognition, or grammatical forms etc. gives these preference over more subtle elements such, for example, as oral expression or insight into the dynamic interaction of different skills, or an elegant use of language. Protests against the domination of teaching by examinations are, however, justified. They protest really against the type and nature of the examination, rather than against having examinations. The remedy is not impossible; the examination should be framed on lines that cannot be crammed for. The teacher does not gain anything for his students if he concentrates only on expected questions. As the examination influences the teaching, we can improve the teaching by improving the examination.

Most tests and examinations at present in use are too comprehensive, those devised by teachers and by official examining bodies like boards and universities are frequently so framed that they attempt to measure to many factors at the same time. For example, a student's mark on a test of translation from English into mother tongue is a composite representing his ability to recognise vocabulary, his use of the context to guess at meaning, his knowledge of Syntax, his background of knowledge of the subject treated in the text and his ability to express himself in his mother-tongue as well as the target language. An examination paper consisting of four or five questions which the student has to answer at length can easily fail to sample more than a small fraction of his knowledge. He may, in fact, have a competence in, say, three quarters of the syllabus. If, however, two of the four questions cover the unknown quarter, he will get less than half marks. If, on the other hand, the examination consists of a large number of smaller items—say a hundred questions—covering the whole of the syllabus equally, lucky shorts are reduced in their effects and ambiguities in the framing of the questions are less important since we have taken a wider and therefore probably more representative sample of the students's knowledge or abilities. Therefore, the existing system of examination should be replaced by the semester system of examination. In some of the universities of India, semester system has already been introduced and it has produced better results as reported by some of the teachers of these universities. The semester system attaches considerable weightage to periodical tests, and home assignments which are an integral part of the evaluation of students's proficiency and achievement. The system of internal assessment as well as continuous evaluating provides the feedback and remedial teaching for improving the teaching/ learning process and also induces students to cultivate regular learning habits.

We have seen that efficient teaching of English in Bihar is lacking also due to the fact that we do not have sufficient number of trained and qualified teachers. Before trying to teach any language, it is incumbent on the part of a teacher to know the system of the language. This brings a teacher closer to the particular language structures. If it is English, then the knowledge of the word-order, the role of structural words, intonation and rhythm are the first requisite of a language teacher. Comparing and contrasting the system of English language with that of the child mother-tongue, a language teacher becomes well-equipped in teaching his subject scientifically. To be a good teacher of English, a person should possess the knowledge of the language and its development, the literature of the language and its growth and the people whose mother-tongue it is and their culture. He should posses adequate knowledge of the language, its complexities and intricacies as well as the latest trends of development in it. He should also have professional knowledge. He should know what different methods and techniques are, what new procedures are being developed, what new instructional material is being devised and what testing devices are evolved. This will require the knowledge of the psychology of learning the language, the psychology of behaviour and educational sociology only with the awareness of the fundamentals of his subject can he be a successful teacher.

English language teaching has become a challenging job. The traditional methods and conservative bases of English language teaching in Bihar are incommensurate to the language needs of the learners. Thus to keep pace with their counterparts in other states of India and the other countries of the world, teachers of English in Bihar must acquaint themselves with latest trend and developments in the field of English language teaching. But at the same time, they should be equipped with necessary materials, professional expertise and resources, such as books, journals and audio-visual aids useful to the teaching of English. If we want to improve the teaching of English in our schools and colleges, it should be seen that only competent teachers of English are appointed for this purpose. Those already in the profession require no less to be informed about the new methods and techniques of teaching English.

Appendices

Appendix I

BHAGALPUR UNIVERSITY, BHAGALPUR

Questionnaire (A)

To School and College students on the problems of teaching English in Bihar.

Dear Students,

We have decided to investigate the problems of teaching English in schools and colleges of Bihar. The purpose of the present study is to complete our research work for Ph.D. degree with your assistance. Your information will be kept confidential. You are requested to send the completed questionnaire latest by the 15th July, 1985.

May I thank you in anticipation of your co-operation.

R.K. Sharma
Dept. of English
Kisan College, Sohsarai
Nalanda-803118

Sohsarai
15.5.1985

How to Answer the Questionnaire

1. Before starting to answer, please go through the questionnaire once carefully.
2. There are two types of items in the questionnaire :
   (a) Those that require descriptive information,
   (b) Those that require a 'yes' or a 'no'.
3. To facilitate recording response to type (b) items a box ☐ is given at the end of such an item, please put a tick (√) for 'yes', and a cross (×) for 'no' in the box.
4. After answering all the items, please go through the questionnaire once again just to make sure.

1. Name of Institution :
2. Student's name :
3. Class :
4. Mother tongue :
5. What is your Father's or guardian's job?
6. What is the highest level of education your father and mother had? Answer the question by putting a tick (√) against the most appropriate answer.

	Father	Mother
College or University		
High School		
Primary School		
I don't know		

7. *(i)* Do you have a radio set at home?

Yes	No

(ii) If your answer in 'yes' how often do you listen to news broadcasts in English?

Always	
Very often	
Sometimes	
Never	

8. *(i)* Do you read newspapers in English?

Yes	No.

(ii) If your answer is 'yes', how often do you read them?

Always

Very often

Sometimes

Never

9. How often do you speak to the following persons in English?

	Always	*Very often*	*Sometimes*	*Never*
Father				
Mother				
Brother/Sister				
Classmates				
Teachers				

10. How often do you borrow books in English from your school/college library to read at home?
11. How often do you write to your friends in English?
12. How often do you go to English films for entertainment?
13. What was the medium of instruction at the following stages of your education?

	Medium of Instruction
From Standard I to V	
Standard VI to X	
In the Class in which you are reading	

14. Besides English, what other languages are you learning now? ....
15. Are the Courses of Study heavy? ....
16. How you learn your lessons? Please try to be accurate as you can. Put a tick ( ) in the box that best describes your method.

	Always	*Sometimes*	*Never*
(i) In my study of English, if I come across a new word, I refer to the dictionary for its meaning.			
(ii) At home, I try to learn by heart the answers to questions on a lesson.			
(iii) I take private tuition in English because I find that the teaching in my school is not sufficient.			
(iv) I find that guides given			

	Always	Sometimes	Never
better help than my teacher's note.			
(v) I try to speak in English to my teachers during English lessons.			

17. The statements given below are opinions of students about the position and importance of English in Education. We would like to know your opinion.

	I agree	I disagree	I don't know
(i) People who speak English are more cultured than those who do not.			
(ii) The development of our country is possible mainly by educated people who know English well.			
(iii) English is no more a language of the British or the American people; it is one of our own national language.			
(iv) Since English is originally not an Indian language, it is very difficult to learn.			
(v) English should not be made a compulsory language of study.			

18. Different people have different reasons for learning English. We want to know what your reasons are.
19. Are you satisfied with the teaching of English by your teacher?
20. Any other information which you would like to give to us.

BHAGALPUR UNIVERSITY, BHAGALPUR

Questionnaire (B)

To the teachers of Schools and Colleges on the problems of teaching English in Bihar.

Dear Sir/Madam,

We have decided to investigate the problems of teaching English in Schools and Colleges of Bihar. The purpose of the present study is to complete our research work for Ph.D. degree with your assistance. Your information will be used only for research purposes and will be kept confidential. You are requested to send the completed questionnaire latest by the 15th July, 1985.

May I thank you in anticipation of your co-operation.

R.K. Sharma
Dept. of English
Kisan College, Sohsarai
Nalanda-803118

Sohsarai
15.5.1985

How to Answer the Questionnaire

1. Before starting to answer, please go through the questionnaire once carefully.
2. There are two types of items in the questionnaire :
   (a) those that require descriptive information,
   (b) those that require a 'yes' or a 'no'.
3. To facilitate recording response to type (b) items a box □ is given at the end of such an item, please put a tick (√) for 'yes', and a cross (×) for 'no' in the box.
4. After answering all the items, please go through the questionnaire once again just to make sure.

1. Name : Mr./Mrs./Miss..
2. Age in years..
3. Name of institution where working now..................
4. Total Teaching experience in years............................
5. How long have you been teaching in the present institution..
6. What is the language you speak at home?..................

7. What was your medium of education—
   (a) at school?
   (b) at College or University?
8. Besides English, in which other language or languages are you able to read and write?

Languages	*Able to read*	*Able to write*
1.		
2.		
3.		

9. What are your educational qualifications?

B.A.	B.Sc.	B.Com.	B.Ed.	M.Ed.
M.A.	M.Sc.	M.Com.	Ph.D.	D.Lit.

10. Have you had any special in-service training in the teaching of English at the secondary level? If 'yes', please give the names and duration of the course or courses :

Name of the Course	*Duration of the Course*
1.	
2.	

11. Is the aptitude for acquiring a foreign language found in your students?
12. Has the growth of love for the mother-tongue been one of the reasons for the decline in the love for English?
13. Are the Courses of Study heavy?
14. Do you lay emphasis on teaching correct pronunciation to the students of your institution?
15. Do you lay emphasis on written work by the students of your institution?
16. Do you lay emphasis on oral practice by the students of your institution?
17. Do you lay emphasis on the correction of mistakes of the students of your institution?
18. What is the position of Grammar teaching in your institution?
19. What are the modes of examination in your institution?
20. What are the modes of evaluation in your institution?

21. What do you think are defects in the teaching of English?
22. Do you generally take the help of teaching aids in your teaching of English?
23. What are your suggestions for improving the courses of study?
24. Are the provisions for lecturing and tutorial work in your institution?
25. What is the method of lecturing followed by you?
26. Have you any criticism to make of the nature of questions set out at the University examinations?
27. Are you satisfied with the evaluation system of today?
28. Are the average students capable of answering critical questions? Is there any advantage in abolishing this kind of questions?
29. Do the students of your institution read books besides the prescribed texts? If not, what is it due to?
30. What are the other problems and their suggestions? Can you point out the problems not covered in the questionnaire?

BHAGALPUR UNIVERSITY, BHAGALPUR

Questionnaire (C)

To the Principals of Schools and Colleges on the problems of teaching English Bihar.

Dear Sir/Madam,

We have decided to investigate the problems of teaching English in schools and colleges of Bihar. The purpose of the present study is to complete our research work for Ph.D. degree with your assistance. Your information will be used only for research purposes and will be kept confidential. You are requested to send the completed questionnaire latest by the 15th July, 1985.

May I thank you in anticipation of your co-operation.

R.K. Sharma
Dept. of English
Kisan College, Sohsarai
Nalanda-803118

Sohsarai
15.5.1985.

How to Answer the Questionnaire

1. Before starting to answer, please go through the questionnaire once carefully.
2. There are two types of items in the questionnaire;
   (a) those that require descriptive information.
   (b) those that require a 'yes' or a 'no'.
3. To facilitate recording response to type (b) items a box (□) is given at the end of such an item. Please put a tick (√) for 'yes', and a cross (×) for 'no' in the box.
4. After answering all the items, please go through the questionnaire once again just to make sure.

(1) Name of the School/College ....

....

(2) Name of the locality..

(3) Type of School/College :
   (i) Privately managed
   (ii) Government aided
   (iii) Government

(4) Medium of instruction :
   English medium
   Regional medium
   Both regional and English medium

(5) Are the school/college premises rented or own?
   ....

(6) Is your institution facing the problem of overcrowded class rooms?

(7) Does your institution possess any of the following audiovisual aids specially for teaching of English :
   (i) Wall charts for teaching composition
   (ii) Phonic cards
   (iii) Tape/Cassette recorder
   (iv) Film Projector
   (v) Slide Projector
   (vi) Radio

(8) Does your institution possess qualified teachers of English?

(9) Whether English is compulsory or optional in your institution?

(10) Who are entitled to offer English methodology in your institution (For the Principals of Training Colleges only)?

(11) Have you got a good library in your institution?

(12) Please give a break up of the student strength this year at your institution in the following columns.

S.N.	*Class where English is taught*	*No. of Students in the class*	*No. of Sections in the class*	*Average No. of students in a section*
I				
II				
III				
IV				
V				

(13) What is the total teacher strength in your institution?

(14) Does your institution publish an annual magazine? If 'yes', does it contain an English section?

(15) What are the other problems and their suggestions? Can you point out the problems not covered in the questionnaire?

Appendix II

SYLLABUSES OF ENGLISH FOR SCHOOLS AND COLLEGES

1. Class VI—Learn English Part-1, Structures 1-55
2. Class VII—Learn English Part-II, Structures 56-110
3. Class VIII—Learn English Part-III, Structures 111-165
4. Classes IX and X—Learn English Part-IV, Stories for Pleasant Reading—A Current Grammer of English, Structures 1-48

Structures 1 to 213
(Classes VI to VIII)

1. This is a (noun).
   This is book/ben/pencil.

2. My
   This is my book.

3. Your
   This is your pen.
4. Adjectives (in attributive position-colour)
   This is red car.
5. Adjectives (size)
   This is a big fox.
6. This (name)
   This is John.
7. I am, you are, He is, She is
   I am your brother.
   You are my sister.
   He is my father.
   She is my mother.
8. X is name of a profession
   Mr. Lal is a teacher.
9. His, Her
   This is his book. This is her beg.
10. 's
    Mr. Das is Mohan's father.
11. That
    That is a bus.
12. Adjectives (predicative)
    She is tall.
13. It
    That is John's kite. It is blue.
14. Question : Is this...? Is that...?
    Is this a car?
    Is that a horse?
    Short answers :
    Yes, it is, No, it isn't
15. Plurals : These/those are....
    This are my dolls.
    Those are his books.
16. Present continuous tense (action word)
    John is running.
17. And
    Leela and Mary are playing.

18. They
    They are my pupils.
19. The
    The Taj is in Agra.
20. Present continuous (with object)
    He is buying a pen.
21. There (introductory)
    There are eight hundred pupils in the school.
22. Imperatives
    Write your name on the black-board.: Come here.
23. Between, under
    Put that chair between the windows.
    Put the basket under the table.
24. Present continuous (give/take-object-to/from-noun)
    The teacher is giving a book to the boys.
    The girls are taking their books from the table.
25. His, them
    Mr. Prasad is near the table. The boys are giving their books to him.
    The children are standing in the playground. Leela is giving biscuits to them.
26. Was, were, wasn't, weren't
    I was at the bus stop.
    Anil and Mohan were in the school.
    He wasn't at the bus stop.
    Mohan and John weren't in the playground.
27. Past tense (full verbs)
    Our school won the match yesterday.
28. Our
    There is big playground near our school.
29. Noun-verb-noun-noun
    The teacher gave mary a book.
30. Her (object)
    Mary's father gave her a book.
31. Time expressions (with prepositions)
    I woke up at six o'clock.

32. Their, Your
    That is their bench.
    These are your pens.
33. Are they/these....?
    Are they your friends?
    Are these your books?
34. Who...?
    Who is your father?
    Who is John's teacher?
35. What....?
    What is this?
    What is he writing?
36. Its
    This is lock. This is its key.
37. We, you
    We are boys; we are walking.
    You are girls; you are sitting.
38. What colour?
    What colour is this book?
39. Has/have (full verbs)
    Mohan has two pencils.
    You have a red bag.
40. In front of, behind
    The chair is in front of the table.
    The chair is behind the table.
41. Where........?
    Where are my books?
42. At
    I am standing at the door.
    The hour hand is at three.
43. Simple future (with will)
    We will go home at 4 o'clock.
44. Shall I/We........?
    Shall I begin the story?
    Shall we sing a song?
45. Of (part of a whole)
    It is the handle of a bag.

This is the handle of a bag.
This is the roof of the house.

46. Have you..........?
Has She/he............?
Have you a pencil?

47. A piece of
This is a piece of chalk/cloth.

48. In the middle of, at the top of, at the bottom of
I am writing my name in the middle of/at the top o
at the bottom of the blackboard.

49. A cup of
A cup of water
A kilo of
A kilo of sugar
A metre of
A metre of silk

50. Next
Ravi is sitting next to Mohan.

51. When................?
When will your examination begin?

52. Or
Give me a pen or a pencil.

53. Can (be able to)
I can lift this table.

54. Ordinals
First, second, third

55. With/without
This is a bag with a handle.
This is a bag without a handle.

Structures Class-VII

56. Questions (simple past)
Did you come to school yesterday?

57. Past progressive
She was making coffee. Her mother was washing th
cups.

58. Questions (with introductory three)
Is there a zoo in your town?

59. Only
    We are three, but there are only two chairs here.
60. Some, any (objective and pronouns with countables)
    I bought some mangoes yesterday.
    Some were good and some were bad.
    Did you buy any orange?
    No, I didn't buy any.
61. One, ones (as pronouns)
    The red book is on the shelf.
    I don't want any red bangles, give me some blue ones.
62. Questions (simple past-negative)
    Did not you inform the police?
63. Every
    The thief opened every box in the room.
64. Present simple (habitual)
    Mr. Prasad wakes up at five o'clock every morning.
65. Always, sometimes, never often (with present simple)
    I always walk to school and sometimes I am late.
66. Before, after (as prepositions)
    Before dinner.
    After breakfast.
67. Question with 'do' (present simple)
    Do you walk to school every day?
68. Where/When question (past tense)
    Where did you go yesterday evening?
    When did you come home yesterday?
69. Where/When question (past tense)
    Where did you go yesterday evening?
    When did you buy this bag?
70. Has got/have got
    he has a car.
    I haven't got a car.
    He has got a cat.
71. Which questions
    Which months have thirty days?
    Which is the power house?

72. Whose, Questions
    Whosc book is his?
    Whose is this?
73. Can (permission)
    You can go now.
74. By
    By bus/train
75. With (meaning together with)
    I am going with my brother Bombay.
76. Some, any (with uncountables)
    Ravi wanted some sugar.
    There wasn't any sugar in the shop.
77. Together
    My brother and I come to school together every day.
78. Present perfect tense
    He has finished his work.
79. Comparative and superlative degree of adjectives (regular)
    Tall, Taller, Talest
80. With, without (instrumental)
    Alexander cut the knot with a sword.
    I can't read without glasses.
81. For noun/pronoun
    I will buy a pen for you.
82. Out of, over (preposition)
    He took a rabbit out of the hat.
    The goat jumped over the fence.
83. For (duration)
    For two hours
84. Another (adjective and pronoun)
    Show me another pen.
    I don't like this pen, can you show me another?
85. Up, down, by (prepositions)
    He climbed up/down the tree.
    We walked by the edge of the lake.
86. How many...............?
    How much...................?

87. (A few, not many, not much)
    I borrowed a few story books from the library.
    There are not many English books in our class.
    There isn't much water in the village tank.
88. The other
    Where are the other boys?
    Where are the others?
89. Both, both the
    Both, the boys are tall.
    They are both tall. Both of them are tall.
    There are houses on both sides of the road.
90. All, all the
    Are all the boys present in class?
    Yes, all are present.
    All animals breathe.
91. Like/want-object
    I like this picture.
    I want a pen.
92. Want/like-infinitive
    He wants to buy a pen.
    I like to collect stamps.
93. Introductory 'it'
    It is a fine day.
    It is six o'clock now.
94. All (adverbial)
    They dressed her all in white.
    Ramu ran all the way to railway station.
    The boys and the girls sang all through the trip.
    All over the garden there were beautiful flowers.
95. Either................or
    Neither..........nor
    You can see me either this evening or tomorrow morning.
    John drinks neither coffee not tea, he drinks only milk.
96. Comparison of adjectives with 'more' and 'most'
    The Olympics were more important than all the other shorter festivals in Greece.
97. Passive voice (present simple, past simple)
    The bell is rung at ten o'clock every day.
    This house was built in 1960.

98. Comparison of adverbs (with 'er' and 'more')
Sita walks slower than her sister. Sita ate more mangoes than her sister.

99. The same, noun
My pen and Ram's pencil are of the same colour.

100. Each other
Gauri and Uma helped each other.

101. Reflective pronoun (objective of preposition, object of verb)
The girl wanten all the toys for herself.
The rat found itself in a trap.

102. Passive voice (future simple)
Gandhiji will always be remembered.

103. Reported commands and requests (with 'asked/told')
The teacher asked Leela to show him her home work.

104. Gerund (as subject and object)
Swimming is a good exercise.
They have stopped speaking to each other.

105. Reported statement principal clause in the present tense and reported statement in all tenses
Sita says she lives in Nagpur.
Sita says she saw her teacher in the park.
Sita says she will come to the picture.

106. Why.......? because..........
Why did you come late? Because I missed the bus.

107. Reported statement principal clause in past simple and statement reported in past simple and past progressive.
He said that he was poor,
My mother said Mohan was learning Hindi.

108. Noun clauses (after-remember, forget, think, know, find, feel, etc.)
I remember that I put my pen in the drawer yesterday.
I know that he is honest.
I found that the bridge was not safe.
I think that it will rain tonight.

109. What noun to verb
Damon did not want Phythias to die.

110. Reported questions : question-word questions; yet, or no
He asked me what my name was.
He asked me if I had a pen.

Structures

111. Must (obligation, duty)
You must obey you parents.
Leela is very ill; we must call the doctor.

112. Have/has to-verb
He has to cook his own food.

113. Past participle (state)
The door is shut; we can't go in.

114. Passive voice (present progressive)
The letter is not ready, it is being typed.

115. Must not, need not
Must I wait for you?
No, you needn't. I will join you at the hotel.
You must not walk on the grass.

116. Question word-infinitive (forming a noun phrase)
I do not know how to swim.
Please tell me where to go.

117. Noun-is/was adjective infinite
The story was easy to read.

118. Become-noun/adjective
When Humaun died, Akbar became king.
On August 15, 1947 India became free.

119. Get adjective
He went out in the rain and got wet.

120. Adverb clauses (with 'when')
When the teacher entered the class, the boys stood up.

121. Too....to
This book is too large to go into my hand bag.

122. Less than
We have written three exercises in less than a week's time.

123. Could, couldn't (past of can)
We could climb the mountain when we were younger.
I could not understand him because he spoke so quickly.

124. Passive voice (past progressive)
The house was being painted.

125. My (possibility)
Please don't go near the dog. It may bite you.

126. May have
The headmistress is not in the school.
She may have gone home.

127. Should (obligation)
You are very ill; you should go to the doctor.

128. Let-noun-verb
I am hungry, let first eat my lunch.

129. Adverbial clause (with 'before')
Leela finishes her home-work before she goes to bed.

130. Infinitive of purpose
He went to the post office to buy some stamps.

131. Adjectival phrase
The tall man with red hair is a doctor.

132. Verb-to-verb
He failed to keep his word.
Remember to lock the gate before you go to bed.

133. Make-objective noun complement.
The boys want to make Ravi Captain.

134. 'How' questions
How do you make this sweet?
How long did you work yesterday?
How much does this pen cost?

135. Fewer than
There are fewer girls than boys in this class.

136. Going-to-verb
We are going to spend holidays in our village.

137. Adjective-infinitive
Eager to learn afraid to go etc.

138. Passive of present perfect
A road has been built, and new buses come to my village.

139. Noun/infinitive
I have some letters to post.

140. Adjectival clauses
The pen that I lost has been found.

141. Not only...............as well
The dams not only save the water of our rivers for irrigation.
They do other things as well.

142. Noun clause
Tell me where the post office is?

143. Present participle in the participal phrases
He came back home bringing the mail.

144. Gerund (after preposition)
Birds fly by flapping their wings.

145. Present participle (attributive)
A moving train. A cheering crowed.

146. Past participle (forming an adjectival phrase)
They went up on a balloon filled with hot air.

147. Used to-verb
We used to buy sugar by the pound, we now buy it by the kilo.

148. Past perfect tense
He didn't know the servant, he hasn't seen him before.

149. Past participle (attributive)
A spoilt child. Boiled rice.

150. Adverbial clauses (with 'as' and 'if')
If it rains, we can't have a gime.
As the rain moved off, my friends waved good-bye to me.

151. Relative clauses (non-defining)
Lal Bahadur Shastri who became Prime Minister of India, was born in a poor home.

152. Noun-verb-noun past participle (object complement)
I found his house locked.

153. Pronoun himself (emphatic)
The emperor led the army himself.
The emperor himself led the army.

154. Adverbial clauses (with 'because' and 'though')
Though he is very old, he is very strong.
I believe it because my father saw it with his own eyes.

155. Advervial clauses (with 'where' and 'so that')
Where there are lot of trees, the air is cool.
Notes this down so that you may not forget.

156. Ought to-verb
We ought to obey our parents.

157. Advervial clauses (with 'since' for reason and 'as' for manner)
Since you say so, I am ready to believe it.
Do as your father tells you to do.

158. Noun clause (as complement)
This is how he became rich.

159. Passive infinitive
Porus wanted to be treated as a king.

160. As-adjective-as
Ashok is not as old as Mohan.

161. Seem infinitive
The sun seems to go round the earth, but it does not.

162. Noun clause (as subject of sentence)
What I tell you is the whole truth.

163. Infinitive as subject
To drive fast on a crowded road may easily cause accidents.

164. As-adverb-as
I shall come back as quickly as I can.

165. Adverbial clause (with 'as soon')
We will leave as soon as we finish our lunch.

Structures Class IX & X

1. Present simple (for future)
I leave for Bombay tomorrow.

2. Question tags
You leave for Bombay tomorrow, don't you?

3. Noun-verb-noun-adjective/past participle
The teacher did not find him eager to learn.
I had my hair cut.

4. It-verb-adjective-noun clause
   It was certain that the man would die.
5. So.....................that adverb clause
   He was so brilliant that he got all the medals for that year.
6. Adverbial clause (with 'as long as')
   As long as I live, I will not forget your kindness.
7. Get-noun/pronoun-to-verb
   He got him to wear a new set of clothes.
8. Present perfect continuous
   I have been talking all the time.
9. Past perfect continuous
   He had been talking all the time and was very tired.
10. Anticipatory 'it'
    It so happened that he fell into a ditch.
11. Some elliptical patterns
    Can the boys go home?
    Yes, if they want to.
    They boy thought he would have a fine time aways from home.
    Boys often think so.
12. Be sure/afraid-noun clause
    I am sure we will win the match.
    I am afraid he will drop those plates.
13. Adverbial clause (with 'unless')
    Unless we take a taxi, we can't get to the station quickly.
14. Had.....................would have
    If they had fought with courage, they would have driven the enemy back.
15. Have got to-verb
    We have got to improve our methods of agriculture.
16. Adverbial clause (comparison)
    He writes better than he speaks.
17. 'Kind of', 'a type of'
    This **kind** of painting I don't understand.
    This **type** of sentence is called a complex sentence.

18. I don't mind-verb-ing
    I don't mind waiting here for an hour.
19. I don't mind-noun/pronoun-verb-ing
    I don't mind-noun coming a little late.
20. Or, otherwise (co-ordinating)
    Work hard, or you will fail.
21. Could/might/ought to-have-verb
    I could have answered all the questions but I hadn't enough time.
    They ought to have given some more time.
22. 'Do' (for emphasis)
    I did bring my pen from home.
    Do tell me, if you want any help.
23. Because of/on account of
    The bus had to stop on account of engine trouble.
24. Since (adverb)
    I haven't seen him since.
25. Else-everything else, anything else, no one else, who else
26. For-noun-infinitive
    This is for you to read in the train.
27. I wish, I were........
28. Had better
    I suppose, I had better tell you.
29. Verb-noun-infinitive (without 'to')
    He saw an apple fall.
30. Prevent/stop-noun-from-gerund
    I prevented Tom going out to play.
31. Adjective-gerund (adverbial)
    He is happy doing his exercise.
    We are happy playing in the sun.
32. Noun clause (in apposition)
    The fact the most dogs are faithful is known to every body.
33. Relative clause (with and preposition)
    This is the house I used to live in.
34. Seem/look, etc. as if,
    He talked as if he knew everything.
    It seemed as if the path would never end.

35. No longer, any longer.
36. Past perfect passive
    We were told the tickets had been sold out.
37. Due to
    The accident was due to the driver's carelessness.
38. Even if...........
    Even if he is very ill, he won't take any medicine.
39. If I were...........
    If I were you, I would be careful about what I said.
    If John were here, he would tell us what do so.
40. 'While' clause (for contrast)
    The policemen numbered barely a dozen while the fighters were more than a hundred.
41. 'Whether' infinitive
    Whether to buy a car or not.
42. In spite of
    In spite of illness, he took the examination.
43. The more.............the more/less
    The more I think of it the more I am convinced.
44. No sooner............
    No sooner had the train arrived than the passengers rushed towards it.
45. Hardly/scarcely........when.....
    Hardly/scarcely had he got up when he began to complain of a pain in his chest.
46. However-adverb or adjective
    However fast he drove, he always had a good control over the car.
47. In case
    Take an umbrella with you in case it rains.
48. Adverbial clause (with 'since')
    Since he left home, he has not written to his mother.

I.A./I.Sc./I.Com. Paper I

Books Prescribed

1. Inter Council Prose Selection
2. Inter Council Poetry Selection

3. Lamb's Tales From Shakespeare
4. Five One Act Plays
5. Tales : Old and new

Paper II

1.	Essay (about 250 words)	14 marks
2.	Letter Writing or Application (about 100-250 words) —	10 "
3.	Comprehension of an unseen Prose passage (about 200 words)	12 "
4.	Expansion of an idea (about 100 words)	10 "
5.	Translation (about 100 words)	10 "
6.	Grammatical items	44 "
		100 marks

Sub. Units

(i)	Articles	4
(ii)	Preposition	4
(iii)	Changing assertive sentence into interrogative	4
(iv)	Active voice/Passive voice	4
(v)	Time and Tense	4
(vi)	Synthesis	3
(vii)	Subject-verb agreement	4
(viii)	Direct and Indirect Speech	4
(ix)	Punctuation	3
(x)	Idioms and Phrases of Common usage	4
(xi)	Common Errors	6
		44

B.A. (Pass) Paper I

(Poetry and Drama)

1. The New Golden Treasury, ed. by R.C. Prasad and M.Q. Towheed (Motilal Banarsidass).

Poems Prescribed

Since There's No Help (Dravton); Poor Soul (Shakespeare); Winter (Shakespeare); All The World's Stage (Shakespeare);

Death-Be Not Proud (Donne); The Pulley (Herbert); On His Blindness (Milton); First Follow Nature (Pope); Tiger (Blake); My Love's Like a Red Red Rose (Burns); The World is Too Much with Us (Wordsworth); To a Skylark (Shelley); She Walks in Beauty (Byron); Ode to the West Wind (Shelley); To The Skylark (Wordsworth); La Belle Dame Sans Merci (Keats); Ode to a Nightingale (Keats); Break, Break, Break (Tennyson); Porphyris's Lover (Browning); Pnilomela (Arnold); Rest (Rosetti); Beauty (Hopkins); Sailing to Byzantium (Yeats); The Hollow Men (Eliot); Look Stranger (Auden).

2. Mac Flecknoe — Dryden
3. Othello — Shakespeare
4. Pyamalion — Shaw
5. Distribution of Marks :
   Explanations out of 8 — 30 marks
   Critical questions — 60 marks
   Prosody and Scansion — 10 marks

Paper II

Miscellaneous Prose

1. Modern Masters (Longman)
   Pieces prescribed : Nos. 2, 5, 6, 7, 8, 9, 10, 11, 12, 15 = 10
2. Representative Short Stories (Motilal Banarsidass)
   Stories Prescribed : 1, 3, 4, 5, 6, 9, 11, 12 = 8
3. Pride and Prejudice Jane Austen
   Distribution of Marks : — 30 marks
4. Explanation out of 8 (from the first two books only)
5. Critical questions (one on each book and the last with alternatives from each of the books) — 60 marks
   Rhetoric — 10 marks

Paper III

Grammar and Composition

Essay — 30 marks
Precis — 15 marks
Expansion (Paragraphy writing) — 10 marks

Common Errors, Blanks, Idioms and Phrases — 25 marks
Pairs of works, Punctuation
Vive-voce Examination — 20 marks

7. B.A. (Hons.) Syllabus yet to come out fully.
8. M.A. (*Patna University*)

Courses of Study
(English)

For Master of Arts Examination, 1983-84

There shall be eight papers in the subject, each carrying 100 marks. Examination in each paper shall be of 4 hours' duration.

The papers shall be divided into three groups. The first five papers shall be identical for groups A and B and shall cover the following periods and subjects :

Paper I — The Renaissance including Drama.
Paper II — The Eighteenth Century (from Dryden to Blake).
Paper III — The Nineteenth Century.
Paper IV — Applied Criticism.
Paper V — Modern Literature.

The remaining papers shall be taken from one of the groups A and B, while for Group C Papers I, II, IV, V and VI will be the same as for Group A. The remaining papers shall cover the following periods and subjects for Group C.

Paper III — The Nineteenth-Century Thought
Paper VII — The Nineteenth-Century Poetry.
Paper VIII — The Nineteenth-Century Fiction.

In lieu of Papers VII and VIII a candidate may offer a thesis carrying 200 marks on a subject approved by the Head of the Department.

GROUP A

Paper VI — Middle English Literature and the History of the English Language.
Paper VII — An essay or essays on the subjects connected with the course.
Paper VIII — Detailed study of a specified literary form or a prescribed author or American Literature of Linguistics.

GROUP B

Paper VI — Descriptive Linguistics.
Paper VII — Historical and Comparative Linguistics.
Paper VIII — Linguistics and the English Grammar.

Primary Teachers Education Colleges

English—Methods and Contents

GROUP A

(1) Principles of Foreign Language Teaching and Learning:
- *(i)* Learning mother tongue versus Foreign Language
- *(ii)* Automatic habit formation
- *(iii)* Psychological aspect of Foreign Language Learning.

(2) Basic skills :
- *(a)* Listening
- *(b)* Speaking
- *(c)* Reading and
- *(d)* Writing

(3) Methods and Technique Teaching :
- *(a)* Grammar and Translation Method
- *(b)* Direct Method
- *(c)* Bilingual Method
- *(d)* Eclectic Method
- *(e)* Playway Method

(4) Teaching material :
- *(i)* Textbooks
- *(ii)* Audio-visual aids, blackboards, Flannel graph, Flash cards, radio, Television, gramophone, records, pictures etc.
- *(iii)* cut out from magazines

(5) Evaluation :
- *(i)* Oral and Written.
- *(ii)* Different types of tests—short answer questions, objective questions and essay type questions.
- *(iii)* Different techniques of measuring linguistic skills.

GROUP B

English-Content Course

(1) Structures:

(a) Basic sentence patterns in English and their modifications and expansions.

(b) First 87 structurcs as listed in New Syllabus for VI and VII.

(2) Vocabulary :

(a) Content and Structural words.

(b) Vocabulary for Active and Passive learning.

(c) Different ways of putting across meaning of words.

(3) Grammar :

(i) Time and Tense

(ii) Determiners

(iii) Expansion of sentence

(iv) Framing questions

(v) Negative

(vi) Prepositions

B.Ed. Course

English

1. Aims of teaching English in India as a second language.
2. Difficulties in learning a foreign language.
3. The Constituents of learning a foreign language :

   (a) The Sound System.

   (b) The Structural Device for Communicating Meaning.

   (c) Vocabulary.
4. The Chief Characteristics of the Structure of English :

   (a) Word-order.

   (b) Use of Structural Words.

   (c) Inflexions.
5. The Signalling System of English :

   (a) Principal form—Classes, Nouns, Verbs, Adjectives, Adverbs.

   (b) The fundamental sentence patterns.

6. The Structural Approach;
   (a) A short review of other methods of teaching English
   (b) A brief discussion of the principles and practices governing the selection, grading and teaching of the language material used in the Readers prescribed in Bihar.
   (c) Oral Work.
   (d) Teaching Through Situation in the Classroom.
   (e) The use of Control especially Controlled Vocabulary throughout.
7. The teaching of reading from the beginning intensively, extensively and for reference.
8. The teaching of Poetry.
   (a) the first three years.
   (b) the last four years.
9. The techniques of teaching grammar with reference to the new syllabus and the exercises in the prescribed books.
10. Testing and Evaluation.

Institute of English, Bihar, Patna

SYLLABUS

(Four-month Course)

A : *English Language and Linguistics*

(a) *Theory*

1. Origin and development of the English language.
2. Attitudes to English grammar, Prescriptive and Descriptive, Transformational or generative grammar, *i.e.* Grammar etc.
3. English Structure :
   3.1. Morphology, Form classes and structure groups
   3.2 Sentence Patterns, Phrase Patterns, Formulas
   3.3 Function units in sentence patterns
   3.4 Syntax
   3.5 Tense
   3.6 Models
   3.7 Punctuation

3.8 Modifications in narration

3.9 Modification in change of voice

3.10 Adverbials

3.11 Question tags and short responses

3.12 Notions of correctness

4. Expressing various concepts, compulsion, obligation, request, permission, prohibition, wish, intention, preference, condition, supposition, probability, determination, willingness, purpose, cause, result, comparison, contrast, concession.
5. Some linguistic terms
6. Linguistics and the Teaching of English

(b) Practice

1. Exercises in Sentence Analysis (Traditional and I.C.).
2. Exercises in Punctuation and Narration.
3. Exercises in sentence construction.

B : *Speech*

(a) *Theory*

1. Speech in relation to writing (including spelling)
2. Speech organs and their functions
3. Cardinal vowels, consonants and vowel-sounds
4. Phenomes and principles of phonetic and phonematic transcription
5. Length, Stress, Rhythm and Intonation
6. Strong and Weak forms
7. Comparison of English and Hindi sounds and Intonation patterns.

(b) *Practice*

1. Exercise in Phonetic Transcription
2. Exercises in reading phonetic script including the use of the Pronouncing Dictionary (Jones)
3. Speech drills (Sounds, rhythm and intonation)
4. Reading from conventional script
5. Transcription from conventional to phonetic script
6. I.P.A. symbols.

C : *English Teaching Methods*

1. Aims, objectives and priorities
2. Some principles of foreign language teaching
3. Selection and grading of materials, vocabulary control
4. Organizing oral work in the class
5. Teaching reading
6. Teaching Grammar
7. Teaching Writing (including spelling)
8. The place of Literature (including poetry) and its teaching in Secondary Schools
9. Language Games
10. Tests and Examinations in English
11. Organising the language class
12. Teaching Aids (including Educational Technology with special Reference to English)
13. Detailed Examination of Structural Syllabus
14. Programme Learning (General and with reference to English)
15. Controlled composition.

Practice

1. Preparing Outlines of Lessons Plans
2. Preparing Teaching Aids
3. Comparing various ELTIs Materials in use.

D. *Viva*

E. Course Assignment
F. Practice Teaching.

Appendix III

THE THREE-LANGUAGE FORMULA IN STATES AND UNION TERRITORIES

N.B.: The statement is given under the following heads :

(a) The first language studied by the large majority of children in the State;

(b) The third language which the children of the State are required to study; and

(c) The second language which the children of the State are required to study.

1. Andhra Pradesh

(a) Telugu.

(b) Telugu for those whose mother tongue is Urdu or Hindi, and Hindi for those whose mother is any language other than Urdu or Hindi—from Class IV—compulsory in Telengana region. Optional in Andhra region in Classes IV and V and compulsory from Class VI.

(c) English from Class III—compulsory.

2. Assam

(a) Assamese.

(b) English from Class IV (which corresponds to Class VI in other States) compulsory.

(c) Hindi from Class IV. Compulsory upto Class VIII, optional upwards.

3. Bihar

No reply received. But it is :

(a) Mother-tongue.

(b) Hindi.

(c) English from Class VI compulsory.

4. Gujarat

(a) Gujarati.

(b) Hindi from Class V. Compulsory.

(c) English from Class VII.

5. Jammu & Kashmir

(a) Urdu (Hindi in Jammu Province).

(b) There seems to be no regular system. Those who have studied Urdu may be taught Hindi and *vice versa* from Class III. Optional.

(c) English from Class VI regularly and in some cases even from Class IV. Compulsory. (It appears that strictly speaking. English is the second language).

6. Kerala

(a) Malayalam.

(*b*) English from Class III. Compulsory.

(*c*) Hindi from Class VI. Compulsory.

7. Madhya Pradesh

(*a*) Hindi.

(*b*) Hindi for those whose mother tongue is not Hindi and a modern Indian language or Sanskrit for those whose mother tongue is Hindi from Class VI. Compulsory.

8. Madras

Not reply received.

9. Maharashtra

(*a*) Marathi.

(*b*) Hindi from Class V. Compulsory.

(*c*) English form Class V. Optional for pupils, but schools must provide for its study.

10. Orissa

(*a*) Oriya.

(*b*) English from Class IV. Compulsory.

(*c*) Hindi from Class VI. Compulsory up to Class VIII and an examination subject up to Class VIII and an examination subject up to Class VIII from 1966.

11. Punjab

(*a*) Hindi in Hindi region and Punjabi in Punjabi region.

(*b*) Punjabi in Hindi region and Hindi in Punjabi region from Class IV. Compulsory.

(*c*) English from Class VI. Compulsory.

12. Rajasthan

(*a*) Hindi.

(*b*) English from Class V, where passing in English is not necessary. Compulsory from Class VI.

(*c*) Minority language (Sindhi, Gujarati, Urdu, Punjabi) or Sanskrit from Class VI. Compulsory, but pass marks are 25 per cent only.

13. Uttar Pradesh

(*a*) Hindi.

(b) English from Class VI under the three-language formula as a compulsory subject. From Class III in selected (16,800) primary schools an optional subject.

(c) A language other than Hindi from the following :

Sanskrit, Urdu, Bengali, Punjabi, Gujarati, Marathi and Tamil.

14. West Bengal

(a) Bengali.

(b) English for those whose first language is Bengali, Hindi for any other language, and Bengali for those whose first language is English—from Class III. Compulsory.

15. Mysore

(a) Kannada.

(b) English from Class V. Compulsory (proposed to be started from Class III).

(c) Hindi from Class VI. Compulsory, but marks are not counted for passing.

(2) The Bihar Gazette, Extra-ordinary No. Patna 375, dated Wednesday, June 7, 1967. Chapter VIII, Paragraph 15.

"A candidate who has obtained pass marks in the aggregate and failed only in English, shall be declared to have passed the Secondary School Examination, without English".

(3) Education Department (Bihar) Notification No. II/B2-01/66E-2553 dated the 13th July, Chapter IX, Paragraph 14.

"A candidate who has not obtained pass marks in English but has obtained pass marks in each of the remaining subjects and also in the aggregate shall be declared to have passed the Higher Secondary School Examination without English. He shall be placed in the division according to total marks obtaine by him in the subject other than English".

Bibliography

(Items listed in the bibliography include books, articles, reports and journals, majority of which are referred to in the footnotes on various pages of this study. There are also a few books, articles and journals listed here which were consulted but not thought of essential to be mentioned in the footnotes.)

Books, Articles and Reports

Agard, F.B. and H.D. Kundel, An Investigation of Second Language Teaching (Boston : Ginn, 1948).

Anand, M.K., The King Emperor's English (Bombay : Hind Kitab, 1948).

Allen, W.S., Living English Speech (London : Longman Group Ltd., 1954).

Ambercrombie, D., 'Teaching Pronunciation' in English Language Teaching, Vol. 3 (1949).

——, Problems and Principles : Studies in the Teaching of English as a Second Language (London : Longmans, Green & Co., 1957).

Allen, H.B. (ed.), Readings in Applied Linguistics (New York: Appleton Century Crofts, 1958).

Basu, A., Education in Modern India (Calcutta : Orient Book Company).

Bhatnagar, Y.C., "Foreign Language Teaching in India : Problems and Prospects" in Mainstream (Februrary 19, 1983).

Browne, H.D., Principles of Language Learning and Teaching (New Jersey: Prentice Hall, 1980).

Burstall, C., Factors Affecting Foreign Language Learning : A Consideration of Some Recent Findings in Language Teaching and Linguistics (Abstracts Vol. 8, No. 1).

Bossing, N.L., Teaching in Secondary Schools (New York : Amerind Publishing Co. Pvt. Ltd., 1970).

Bose, K., Teaching of English : A Modern Approach (Delhi: Doaba House, 1979).

Broughton, G.C. Brumfit, K. Flavell, P. Bill and A. Pincas, Teaching English as a Foreign Language (London : Routledge and Kegan Paul, 1978).

Bansal, R.K., The Intelligibility of Indian English (CIEFL : Monograph, No. 4, 1969).

——, Introduction to English Language Teaching : Vol. 2, Phonetics and Spoken English (Delhi : OUP, 1978).

Banerjee, S.N., Lord Macaulay and Higher Education in India (Calcutta : I.C. Bose, 1978).

Bennet, W.A., Aspects of Language and Language Teaching (London: Cambridge University Press, 1967).

Bialystok, E. and M. Frohlich. 'Aspects of Second Language Learning in Classroom Settings', Working Papers on Bilingualism 13/1 (1977).

Belasco, S., 'The Feasibility of Learning a Second Language in an Uncultural Situation' in P. Pmsleuz and T. Quinn (eds.), 1971.

Bram, J., Language and Society (New York : Doubleday, 1955).

Bruton, J.C., 'Some Misconceptions about the English and about Language Teaching Current in India' in Bulletin of the CIEFL No. 1 (Hyderabad : September 1961).

Chib, S.N., Language, Universities and Nationalism in India (Mysore : Oxford University Press, 1936).

Chatterji, S.K., The Cultural Heritage of Indian Vol. V, 'Language and Literatures' (Calcutta : Ram Krishna Mission, 1978).

Carrol, J.B. and S. Sapan, Modern Language Aptitude Test (New York : Psychological Corporation, 1959).

Catford, J.C., 'The Teaching of English as a Foreign Language' in Randolph Quirk and A.H. Smith (eds.), (1964).

——, The Teaching of English (London : Secker and War-burgh, 1959).

Corder, S. Pit., English Language Teaching and Television (London: Longmans, 1960).

Clarke, M.A., 'Second Language Acquisition as a Clash of Consciousness' in Language Learning 2612 (1981).

Christopherson, Paul, Second Language Learning : Myth and Reality (Harmondsworth : Penguin Books, 1973).

Derrick June, Teaching English to Immigrants 'Organiser Schools Council Project in English for Immigrant Children', London (1966).

Dulay, H. and M. Burt (eds.), Second Language Learning Teaching : A Scientific Approach (New York : McGraw Hill, 1964).

Ezekiel, N., Presidential Address at the 35th Session. AIETC, Pune (1984).

Fathman, A., 'The Value of Morpheme Order Studies for Second Language Learning' : Working Papers in Bilingualism (Toronto No. 18).

Faucett. L., The Teaching of English in the Far East (Harrap, 1938).

Feenstra, H.J., Aptitude, Attitude and Motivation in Second Language Acquisitions, Dissertation, University of Western Ontario, (1964).

Gandhi, M.K., The Problem of Education (Ahmedabad : Navajivan Press, 1962).

——, Young India (1919-22).

Gatherer, W.A., A Study of English (London : Heinemann Educational Books, 1980).

Gokak, V.K., English in India : Its Present and Future (Bombay; Asia Publishing House, 1964).

Gardner, R.C. and W. Lambest, Attitudes and Motivation in Second Language Learning (Rowely Mass : Newbury House, 1972).

Genesse, F., 'The Role of Intelligence in Second Language Learning' in Language Learning Vol. 26, No. 2.

Guiora, A.Z., 'Language and Person : Studies in Language Behaviour' in Language Learning Vol. 25, No. 1.

Gatenby, E.V., 'The Training of Language Teachers in W.R. Lee (ed.) E.L.T. Selections II (London : Oxford University Press, 1967).

Gandhi, Indira, 'Speech on 15 August, 1967' reported in The Times of India (Delhi, 16 Augst, 1967).

Halliday, M.A.K., A. McIntosh and P. Strevens, The Linguistic Sciences and Language Teaching (London : ELBS 2, Longman Group Ltd., 1966).

HIll, L.A., A Guide to Correct English (London : Oxford University Press, 1965).

Hill, W.H., Improvement of Examinations (Calicut; University of Calicut, 1972).

Haycraft, J., An Introduction to English Language Teaching (London: Longman, 1978).

Henle, P. (ed.), Language, Thought and Culture (Ann Arbor, Michigan, OUP (1958).

James, H.R., Education and Statesmanship in India 1797-1910 (London : Longmans, 1952).

John, V.V., Presidential Address at the All India English Teachers Conference (1967).

Jokobovits, L., 'Implications of Recent Psycholinguistic Developments for the Teaching of a Second Language' in Language Learning Vol. 18, Nos. 1 & 2 (June 1968).

Kachru, B.B., The Indianization of English : The English Language in India (Delhi : Oxford University Press, 1983).

Kral, T.J., 'Teaching Pronunciation' (While seeming to be doing something else) in English Teaching Forum, Vol. XVIII No. 2 (April, 1980).

Lado, R., Linguistics Across Cultures (Ann Arbor : University of Michigan Press, 1957).

——, and C.C. Fries, English Pronunciation : Intensive Course in English (AnnArbor : Michigan, OUR, (1958).

Lugton, R.C. (ed.), English as a Second Language : Current Issues (Philadelphia : Centre for Curriculum Development, 1970).

Mackey, W.F., Language Teaching Analysis (London : Longmans, Green and Comp. Ltd., 1966).

Marckwarelt, H.A., Linguistics and the Teaching of English, Indiana University Press, (Bloomington, London, 1966).

MacCarthy, P.H.D., Talking of Speaking : Papers in Applied Phonetics (London : Oxford University Press, 1972).

Nagarajan, S., The Decline of English in India, A Historical Perspective in College English 43/7, (1981).

Naiman, N.M., M. Frohlich, and H.H. Stern, The Good Language Learner (Toronto : Ontario Institute for Studies in Education, 1978).

Nihalani, P., R.K. Tongue, and P. Hosali, Indian and British English : A Handbook of Usage and Pronunciation (Delhi : OUP, 1979).

Pride, J.B., 'Communicative Needs in the Learning and Use of English' in Indian Journal of Applied Linguistics. Vol. IV, No. 2 (June 1978).

Pimsleur, P., Language Aptitude Battery (New York : Harcourt Brace & World, 1968).

Paffard, M., Thinking About English (London : Wordlock Educational, 1978).

Pattison, B., 'Some Notes on the Teaching of Literature' in ELT

Selections (ed.) W.R. Lee (London : Oxford University Press, 1967).

Pandit, P.B., 'Indian Readjustments in Indian Linguistics.

Parliamentary Paper 1852-53 XXXII.

Palmer, H.E., The Scientific Study and Teaching of Language (London : Harrap, 1917).

Pilliner, A.F.G., 'Subjective and Objective Testing', in Alan Davies (ed.) Language Testing Symposium : A Psycho-linguistic Approach (London : Oxford University Press, 1968).

Quinn, T. and Pimsleur (eds.), The Psychology of Second Language Learning (Cambridge : Cambridge University Press, 1971).

Report of the Secondary Education Commission (Government of India, 1956).

Report of Indian Education Commission (Government of India, 1883).

Report of Official Language Commission (Government of India, 1952).

Report on Medium of Instruction (University Grants Commission, 1961).

Report of Bihar State Secondary Education Committee Government of Bihar, 1962).

Report of English Review Committee (University Grants Commission, 1965).

Report of Secondary Education Commission (Government of India, 1972).

Report for the year 1984-85 (Education Department, Government of Bihar).

Report on Standards of University Education (University Grants Commission, (1965).

Richards, J.C. (ed.), Understanding Second and Foreign Language Learning (Longman, 1974).

Sharp, H. (ed.), Selections from Educational Records, (Calcutta : Superintendent of Government Printing, 1920).

Sharma, G.R., The Teacher of Hindi in Shiksha (April, 1957).

Sharma, P.K., Aspects of English Language Teaching in India (Bhagalpur : Bharat Book Depot, 1985).

——, 'The Art of Writing Lesson in English for Correspondence Course' in B.K. Sinha (ed.), Sesson Writing for Correspondence Students (Institute of Correspondence Courses, Patna University, Patna, 1982).

Sinha, S.P., English in India—A Historical Study with particular reference to English Education in India (Patna : Janaki Prakashan, 1978).

Spolsky, B., 'Recent Research in TESOL', TESOL Quarterly, 2, (1968).

Syllabus for Middle/High Schools (Education Department, Government of Bihar, 1979).

Syllabus for Primary Teachers Education Colleges (Education Department Government of Bihar, 1977).

——, Spoken Language (London : Longmans, Green and Co., 1956).

Srivastav, R.C. and K. Bose, Theory and Practice of Teacher Education in India (Allahabad : Chugh Publications, 1978).

Stern, H.H., Foreign Language in Primary Education (London : OUP, 1967).

Thakur, D., B. Ranjan and S.D. Sinha, Learn English Book I, Patna : (Bihar State Text Book Publishing Ltd., 1981).

Thakur, D. and P. Thakur, "The Recognition of Vocabulary of P.U.C. Students in Bihar : A Reference Manual for Text Book Writers' Paper presented at the Five Day Seminar on Materials Production CIEFL, Hyderabad (February 1975).

Taylor, H.J.S., 'Making the most of a Text-book Passage' in ELTJ 25/2 (1971).

Thyne, J.M., The Psychology of Learning and Techniques of Teaching (London : University of London Press, 1963).

Valette, R., Modern Language Testing (New York : Harcourt Brace, Jovanovich, 1977).

Vidomec, V., Multilingualism (Leyden : A.W. Sythoff, 1963).

Wardt, L.H.M., Linguistics and Teaching of English (Bloomington : London : Indiana University Press, (1966).

Wright, E. and C. Ramsay, Lage and Second Language Learning in Journal of Social Psychology (Vol. 94).

Wyatt, The Teaching of English in India (London : Clarendon Press, 1950).

Wilkins, D.A., Linguistics in Language Teaching (London : Edward Arnold, 1974).

Wingard, P., 'Training English Lecturers in an Overseas University' in R.R. Jordon (ed.), Case Studies in ELT (London : Collins ELT, 1913).

West, M., The Teaching of English : A Guide to the New Method Series (London : Longmans, 1953).

Wertheimer, M. and Scherar, G., A Psycholinguistic Experiment in Foreign Language Teaching (New York : McGraw-Hill, 1964).

Wright, A., Audio-Visual Materials in Language Teaching in J.P.B. Allen and S. Pit Corder (eds.) (1974).

Yardi, V.V., 'Teaching English as a Third Language : Some Theoretical Considerations' in Forum XVI, 2 (1978).

Journals

British Journal of Educational Psychology, London (U.K.).

British Journal of Language Teaching (Oxford, U.K.).

Canadian Journal of Linguistics (Toronto and Montreal, Canada).

The Candadian Modern Language Review (Toronto, Canada).

CIEFL Bulletin—A Research Journal—Published Half Years (Hyderabad, India).

CIEFL News Letter—A Quarterly devoted to ELT Activities (Hyderabad, India).

English Language Research Journal (Burmingham, U.K.).

English Language Teaching (London, U.K.).

English Language Abstracts (London, U.K.).

English Teaching Forum (Washington, D.C., U.S.A.).

Indian Journal of Applied Linguistics (New Delhi, India).

International Review of Applied Linguistics in Language Teaching (Heidelberg, Germany).

Journal of Linguistics (Cambridge, U.K.).

Language Forum : A Quarterly Journal of Language and Literature (New Delhi, India).

Language Learning : A Journal of Applied Linguistics (Michigan, U.S.A.).

Modern English Teacher (London, U.K.).

Modern Language Teacher (London, U.K.).

Practical English Teaching (London, U.K.).

Teaching English (Calcutta, India).

Teaching English as a Second Language Reporter (Lale, Hawai).

TESL Talk : Quarterly For Teachers of English as a Second Language (U.S.A.).

Index